# What Type of College for What Type of Student?

Albert B. Hood

BASED UPON RESEARCH CONDUCTED BY
ALBERT B. HOOD AND EDWARD O. SWANSON

UNIVERSITY OF MINNESOTA PRESS, Minneapolis

PRINTED IN THE UNITED STATES OF AMERICA AT
THE LUND PRESS, INC., MINNEAPOLIS

Library of Congress Catalog Card Number: 68-65220

PUBLISHED IN GREAT BRITAIN, INDIA, AND PAKISTAN BY THE OXFORD UNIVERSITY PRESS,
LONDON, BOMBAY, AND KARACHI, AND IN CANADA BY THE COPP CLARK
PUBLISHING CO. LIMITED, TORONTO

# ACKNOWLEDGMENTS

THIS STUDY would not have been possible without the cooperation of hundreds of Minnesota educators. All the data necessary to this research study were collected either in conjunction with or as a part of the Statewide Testing Program operated by the Student Counseling Bureau at the University of Minnesota and supported by the Association of Minnesota Colleges. The assistance of the principals and counselors in all the secondary schools of the state who administered the questionnaires and the help of the registrars in Minnesota colleges who provided follow-up information is greatly appreciated.

Particular tribute must be paid to the many contributions of Dr. Edward O. Swanson — as a colleague in formulating the initial plans for the project, as a co-investigator in carrying out the study, and as the staff member of the Statewide Testing Program who provided both the support of that staff and the large amounts of information available in that agency.

Dr. Ralph F. Berdie, the former director of the Student Counseling Bureau, deserves mention not only for his support and consultation, but for his major contributions to a prior study on which this investigation was based. Other members of the staff of the Student Counseling Bureau also contributed many helpful suggestions, and Dean Edmund G. Williamson of the University of Minnesota gave his support which was important to carry out this research.

A great deal of effort goes into tabulating and analyzing information gathered for a study such as this and the contributions of the following individuals should be acknowledged: David Seaquist and Mary Johannson were responsible for much of the statistical analysis of the information collected in this study. Douglas Elliott, Christopher Smith, and Robert Peterson did all the necessary data processing and computer programming. James Robertson, Roy Cedarholm, and John Viesselman completed innumerable calculations in the analysis of the data. Beverly Crow and Christine Fossum executed much of the typing and clerical work connected with the project. Deanna Berkenpas did many tabulations and, along with Gertrude Nidey, was also responsible for typing the manuscript.

Appreciation is also expressed to the U.S. Office of Education of the Department of Health, Education, and Welfare for the financial support which made this study possible through Cooperative Research Project No. 2182 (OE-4-10-014).

# TABLE OF CONTENTS

# WHAT TYPE OF COLLEGE
# FOR WHAT TYPE OF STUDENT?

## Chapter 1

# PROBLEMS IN EVALUATING COLLEGE CHOICE

THE COLLEGE-BOUND student of today has a wide range of types and sizes of colleges from which to choose. He can choose a liberal arts college, a state college, a state university, a private university, or a junior college. The college he chooses can be large or small, urban or rural, public or private, secular or nonsecular, coeducational or limited to one sex, within commuting distance from his home or across the continent.

The students themselves come from all types of social, economic, and cultural backgrounds. Some are from wealthy families and a few from poverty-stricken environments; some are from isolated farms, others from large metropolitan and suburban areas. They differ widely in personality characteristics and in factors such as ability, previous achievement, motivation, attitudes, and values. Many are from the top 5 percent of their high school class, but a few are from the bottom 5 percent. Some are relaxed and easygoing while others are anxious and tense; some are socially adept, others socially inept. Their reasons for attending college, their attitudes toward the college, and their educational goals vary widely.

With such great variance in both colleges and students, some colleges must be better than others for certain students. The problem is — what types of colleges for what types of students? Would a high-ability student from a low socioeconomic background be more successful attending a small residential liberal arts college or commuting to a public junior college? Given three students of equal ability and similar backgrounds, one very outgoing and socially adept, the second introverted and shy, and the third a rebellious nonconformer, which one should attend the large college and which the small, which should commute and which should go away to college?

This book examines the academic success of different college students in different types of colleges. While academic success is only one aspect

3

of a successful college career, it is crucial both for remaining in college and for gaining admission to graduate and professional schools. Furthermore, it is the only criterion of college success available on most campuses.

After students enter college their achievement varies widely at all levels of ability. An estimated 50 percent of them drop out before graduation and for a large portion of dropouts, poor grades are related to their leaving. The greatest loss to society of high-ability young people not trained to their fullest potential is now occurring at the college level. At one time this "talent loss" occurred primarily among able students leaving high school before graduation. More recently it was primarily due to the large number of able students graduating from high school but not continuing their education beyond that point. Efforts by society to reduce this talent loss have resulted in comprehensive high school guidance programs and national programs of scholarships and loans to college-bound students. These programs have been quite successful with the result that most able young people now undertake some form of post-high-school education. Information that helps match students to colleges which they are likely to find compatible and where they are likely to be successful will be useful to both the individual and society.

## Considerations in Choice of College

The student choosing a college usually asks questions such as these: "Will I be admitted?" "Can I afford it?" and sometimes "Does it offer the kinds of studies which lead to the career I wish to pursue?" "Is it the sort of college I want to attend?" In answer to these questions the student considers cost, quality of student body, certain aspects of the curriculum, and perhaps sex of student body, size, religious affiliation, and geographical location. Other factors which he may or may not consider include prestige or reputation, strength of major departments, extracurricular activities, living accommodations, social life, opportunity for independent study, athletics, financial aids available, and social or intellectual attitudes of the students. In addition, college choice should be related to other values and goals in life such as marriage, plans for graduate work, and career plans. A wide range of colleges probably are suitable for many students — an individual should not decide that only one college is best for him.

Although the choice of a college is obviously an important decision, in many cases the choice is made in a haphazard manner. Often it is

nade because of the influence of friends or parental pressure, or as a result of a brief visit to the campus. Frequently it is made without considering available alternatives or else is made on the basis of incorrect
or incomplete information. Sometimes the choice is a good one, but in
many cases a more thoughtful selection would have resulted in a hap-
pier choice. Studies of National Merit Scholarship finalists have shown
that even the most talented students frequently use sloppy thinking in
selecting colleges, which often results in unhappiness and transfer (For-
rest, 1961).

Sometimes strong feelings about attending a private college reflect
the opinion that such colleges provide a higher quality of education
than public ones; strong feelings about a small college grow out of the
idea that more personal attention will produce greater achievement.
Preference for a church-controlled institution may be based on the assumption that stronger religious values will result; or a single-sex institution may be preferred because of the feeling that distractions inherent
in the coeducational situation lead to a lower level of scholastic achievement. For some, such as the baby wearing the sweat shirt labeled "Dart-
mouth '88," the decision may be made years before college age is reached
— given a high level of secondary school achievement and continued parental affluence. Often a student chooses a particular college because of
an unusual program there or because of the reputation of a particular
department in which he plans to major. A change of vocational goal frequently is accompanied by disillusionment with the college originally
selected. One of the principal reasons given by transferring students is
a change in their major field of study.

The whole question of satisfaction with choice of college poses yet
another difficult problem — often students become dissatisfied with the
intellectual or social climate of the institution at which they enroll. In
the studies reported, approximately 85 percent of students say they are
satisfied with the college they chose and would not choose any other.
This figure, however, is in conflict with other statistics showing that approximately half of the students who enter a particular college either
drop out or transfer to another college. An extensive study by Rand
(1966) yielded little information on this topic in spite of the fact that
student satisfaction was examined for students with various personality
and attitudinal characteristics in different types of institutions. Perhaps a more sensitive measure of satisfaction than that resulting from
the typical questionnaire item asking whether or not the student is sat-

isfied would yield more useful information on this subject. Such a questionnaire item is usually multiple choice with four or five levels of satisfaction and most students indicate high satisfaction.

However, even if a useful measure of satisfaction is derived and various characteristics of students are found to be related to satisfaction, there would still be the question of the extent to which a student might be better off attending a college where he feels some dissatisfaction. Most colleges do not place a very high value on admitting or graduating happy and complacent young adults. On the contrary, most colleges attempt to challenge values, to develop concerns for humanitarian, political, and international causes, and to make students aware of the inadequate information available in various fields — all goals that may produce dissatisfied graduates.

Another consideration in selecting a college might be the impact a particular college would be likely to have on a particular student. Very little is known about this at the present time. Several researchers have given considerable attention to the measurement of different college environments; others are attempting to assess the impact colleges have on students. It will be some time before we will know anything about the differential impact of varying college environments on particular students.

## Purpose of This Investigation

Although the problem of matching students with colleges is a complex one, most people agree that the majority of students will be better off in colleges where they have a reasonable chance of succeeding. The most appropriate college may not be the one where the student will be the most successful, but neither should he attend a school where he is certain to fail. Beyond that point, however, things are not so simple.

In this book a number of background and personality characteristics of students who attended various types of colleges will be examined along with their academic achievement. But college choice should not simply be a matching of characteristics of the student with those of a typical entering freshman class in a particular college. Little is known about the effects on either motivation or achievement of being part of a homogeneous group, and furthermore, most students are not looking for a chance to spend four years with persons just like themselves.

Academic achievement as measured by college grade-point average has been used as the measure of college success in this study. Such an index measures only a very small proportion of the many aspects which constitute a successful college career. Although the importance of grades cannot be overlooked since minimal grade-point averages must be maintained to remain in a given college and they are important for entrance into professional and graduate schools, nevertheless, most studies of success after college, and success outside of the classroom, show practically no relationship to college grades. The fact that grade-point average was the only criterion of achievement in college that was available suggests the need for colleges to attempt to delineate additional areas in which to evaluate their students.

It is expected that the reader of this book is familiar with the widely differing ability levels of students found both within a given institution and among various institutions — information found in such publications as Sanford's *The American College* (1962), *Manual of Freshman Class Profiles* (1964) published by the College Entrance Examination Board, and various norms and expectancy tables available for many colleges.

Chapter 2

# A STATEWIDE SURVEY OF COLLEGE ACHIEVEMENT

▀▀▀▀▀▀▀▀▀▀▀▀▀▀▀▀▀▀▀▀▀▀▀▀▀▀▀▀▀▀▀▀▀▀▀▀▀▀▀▀▀▀▀▀▀▀▀▀▀▀▀▀▀▀

THIS STUDY was possible because a great deal of information could be assembled on an entire statewide population of college-bound students. Questionnaire and test data had been collected on almost all (97 percent) the students who graduated from Minnesota high schools, both public and private, in 1961. In addition, first-year college grades were gathered for all those students who entered Minnesota colleges as freshmen in the fall of 1961.

## Questionnaire Data

Information on family, economic, cultural, and social backgrounds was available from a questionnaire filled out by these Minnesota students in their high schools in January of their senior year. This questionnaire, entitled "After High School — What?" (see pages 9–12), had been developed in an earlier study (Berdie, 1954) to relate personal background factors to students' post-high-school plans. In that study, comparisons had been made between information provided by students on the questionnaire and information obtained from parents in interviews. The data provided by these items appeared reliable. For the present study several changes were made in the questionnaire, including the addition of twenty-nine personality items. Of these, twenty-five were the highest validity items from the social relations and conformity scales of the Minnesota Counseling Inventory (Berdie and Layton, 1953).

## Test Scores, Percentile Ranks, and College Grades

High school percentile ranks and scores on a scholastic aptitude test were available for almost all the 1961 graduates. Under the sponsorship of the Association of Minnesota Colleges, which pays for the program, the Student Counseling Bureau of the University of Minnesota admin-

# UNIVERSITY OF MINNESOTA
## OFFICE OF THE DEAN OF STUDENTS
### STUDENT COUNSELING BUREAU

H.S. _____ 1-3

Iden. No._____ 4-6

## After High School—What?
### For High School Seniors
### 1961

In order to provide information about what high school seniors are planning for the next year and to show the reasons for these plans, you are being asked to answer the questions below.

Write in the answer or place a check mark (√) before the appropriate word or phrase.

7-20. Name (Print)_____

                         **Last**                      **First**               **Middle**

21. (1)_____Male (2) _____Female

2-23. Age last birthday_____ years

24. Occupation of father: (Check the item which applies)

(1)_____Profession (lawyer, banker, doctor, teacher, minister, dentist, etc.)

(2)_____Owns or manages business (store, gas station or garage, photography or barber shop, insurance agency, hotel or cafe, repair shop, newspaper, etc.)

(3)_____Office work (bookkeeper, cashier, postal clerk, etc.)

(4)_____Sales (insurance, real estate, retail store, etc.)

(5)_____Owns or manages farm

(6)_____Skilled tradesman (carpenter, electrician, machinist)

(7)_____Factory worker (laborer, farm laborer, janitor, mine laborer)

(   ) Other occupations: (Be specific)

_____
                    **(Write in name of occupation)**

25. Education of father: (Check highest level attained)

(1)_____Did not attend school

(2)_____Some grade school

(3)_____Completed eighth grade

(4)_____Some high school

(5)_____Graduated from high school

(6)_____Business or trade school

(7)_____Some college work (including teacher training)

(8)_____Graduated from college

(9)_____Holds more than one college degree

26. Education of mother: (Check highest level attained)

(1)_____Did not attend school

(2)_____Some grade school

(3)_____Completed eighth grade

(4)_____Some high school

(5)_____Graduated from high school

(6)_____Business or trade school

(7)_____Some college work (including teacher training)

(8)_____Graduated from college

(9)_____Holds more than one college degree

27. Which of the following ways best describes how your family gets its income? (Check the one phrase which best applies)

(1)_____Professional fees or business profits (Including profits from farms)

(2)_____Fixed salary (Paid on a monthly or yearly basis)

(3)_____Wages (Paid on an hourly or daily basis and depending on number of hours worked)

(4)_____Income from investments (Stocks, bonds, real estate, insurance)

(5)_____Pensions (Government or other)

28. Check the phrase which best describes your family's income:

(1)_____Frequently have difficulty making ends meet

(2)_____Sometimes have difficulty in getting the necessities

(3)_____Have all the necessities but not many luxuries

(4)_____Comfortable but not well-to-do

(5)_____Well-to-do

(6)_____Wealthy

29. Course or curriculum taken in high school: (Check the one which best describes your course)

(1)_____Commercial (2)_____Agriculture (3)_____Shop or Technical (4)_____College Preparatory (5)_____General

(   ) Other_____
                                   **(Write in)**

30-31. Check the most important reason or reasons why you originally selected the course you checked in item 29:

30
(1)_____Only one offered in school
(2)_____Teacher's advice
(3)_____Counselor's advice
(4)_____Parent's advice
(5)_____Required to by school
(6)_____Brothers or sisters took it
(7)_____Seemed easiest
(8)_____Required by parents

31
(1)_____Was best in this work
(2)_____Fitted vocational plans best
(3)_____Course seemed most interesting
(4)_____Friends took it
(5)_____Brother's or sister's advice
(6)_____"Everyone else" took it
(7)_____Don't know
(    ) Other_____
(Write in)

32-33-34. What are your plans for next year (1961-1962)? (Check the one plan you are now most seriously considering)

32
(1)_____Get a job_____
(2)_____Work for parents_____
(3)_____Go to college_____
(4)_____Go to trade school_____
(5)_____Go to business school_____
(6)_____Go to other school_____
(7)_____Do postgraduate work in high school
(8)_____Enter the Military Service
(9)_____Other_____
(Write in)

33-34
If yes, what kind of work?_____
If yes, what kind of work?_____
If. yes, which college?_____
If yes, which school?_____
If yes, which school?_____
If yes, which school?_____

35-36. Check the reasons for making the plans you indicated above:

35
(1)_____To prepare for a vocation
(2)_____To be with old school friends
(3)_____To get a liberal education
(4)_____To start making money quickly
(5)_____To please parents or friends
(6)_____To be independent
(7)_____To make friends and helpful connections

36
(1)_____It is "the thing to do"
(2)_____Foregone conclusion, never questioned why
(3)_____Will enable me to make more money
(4)_____"Everyone here" does this
(5)_____Tired of studying, have had enough education
(6)_____Only thing I can afford to do
(7)_____Like school
(8)_____ Other_____
(Explain)

37. Has marriage or the early prospect of marriage influenced your plans for the coming year?
(1)_____Yes  (2)_____No

38. In your present thinking, have you any idea when you plan to get married?
(1)_____Already married
(2)_____This year
(3)_____Next year
(4)_____In a few years
(5)_____Can't say
(6)_____Not planning on marriage

39. If you are going to college next year (1961-1962), to what extent will your family help you pay expenses?
(1)_____Pay all my expenses
(2)_____Pay most of my expenses
(3)_____Pay some of my expenses
(4)_____Pay none of my expenses

40. If you are not going to college, would you change your plans and attend college if you had more money?
(1)_____Yes  (0)_____No

41. If you checked "Yes" to the last item, how much more money would you need to attend college?
(1)_____Enough to pay all my expenses
(2)_____Enough to pay about half my expenses
(3)_____Enough to pay less than half my expenses

42. If you are not going to college, could you afford to go if you wished to go?
(1)_____Could afford it easily
(2)_____Could barely afford it
(3)_____Could afford it but it would involve many sacrifices
(4)_____Could not afford it

10

**43.** How does your family feel about your going to college?

(1)_____Insists that I go

(2)_____Wants me to go

(3)_____Is indifferent

(4)_____Doesn't want me to go

(5)_____Won't allow me to go

**44.** If you are planning on college, are you considering any graduate or professional training after your undergraduate college work?

(1)_____Yes  (0)_____No    If "Yes," indicate type_____

**45.** If you are not going to college next year, do you plan to go at some later date?

(x)_____No

_____Yes (If you checked "yes" here, indicate when you plan to attend college):

(1)_____After 1 year    (2)_____After 2 years    (3)_____After 3 years    (4)_____After 4 or more years

**46.** Do you have a furnace or central heating in your home?

(1)_____Yes  (0)_____No

**47.** Do you have running water in your home?

(1)_____Yes  (0)_____No

**48.** Do you have both hot and cold running water?

(1)_____Yes  (0)_____No

**49.** Do you have an electric or gas refrigerator?

(1)_____Yes  (0)_____No

**50.** Do you have a telephone in your home?

(1)_____Yes  (0)_____No

**51.** Does your family own or rent a deep freeze unit or a locker?

(1)_____Yes  (0)_____No

**52.** Do you have electric lights in your home?

(1) _____Yes  (0)_____No

**(Items 53-59 in next column)**

**53.** Do you have a television set in your home?

(1)_____Yes  (0)_____No

**54.** Does your family own your home?

(1)_____Yes  (0)_____No

**55.** How many people live in your home?_____(    )

**56.** How many rooms are there in your home excluding the bath room?_____(    )

**57.** How many people excluding yourself sleep in your room?_____(    )

**58.** How many passenger cars does your family own? (Check)
0_____  1_____  2 or more_____

**59.** What is the year and make of your family's newest car?
Year_____  Make_____ (    ) (    )

**60.** Do you live on a farm? (1)_____Yes  (0)_____No

**61.** If you live on a farm, have you had a major responsibility for a part of its management?

(1)_____Yes  (0)_____No

**62.** If you live on a farm, is there a place for you in its operation which would provide a good future for you if you should wish to stay?

(1)_____Yes  (0)_____No

**63.** Approximately how many books does your family have in your home? (Check appropriate category)

(1)_____ 0- 9    (3)_____25-49    (5)_____100-up

(2)_____10-24    (4)_____50-99

**64-65-66.** Which of these magazines does your family subscribe to or regularly buy?

**64**

(1)_____Reader's Digest

(2)_____Life

(3)_____Saturday Evening Post

(4)_____Look

(5)_____McCall's Magazine

(6)_____Ladies Home Journal

(7)_____Better Homes and Gardens

(8)_____Good Housekeeping

(9)_____American Home

(0)_____Coronet

(x)_____Farm Journal

**65**

(1)_____Redbook

(2)_____National Geographic Magazine

(3)_____Time

(4)_____True

(5)_____Parents' Magazine

(6)_____Capper's Farmer

(7)_____Argosy

(8)_____Popular Mechanics

(9)_____Popular Science

(0)_____Newsweek

(x)_____Successful Farming

**66**

(1)_____U. S. News & World Report

(2)_____Sports Afield

(3)_____Sports Illustrated

(4)_____Holiday

(5)_____New Yorker

(6)_____Fortune

(7)_____The Farmer

(8)_____Atlantic Monthly

(9)_____Harper's

**67.** Others_____

11

**68-69-70.** To which of these organizations does your father or mother or both belong?

68
- (1)_____P.T.A. or Mothers' Club
- (2)_____American Legion or VFW
- (3)_____Rotary
- (4)_____Knights of Columbus
- (5)_____Elks
- (6)_____Masons
- (7)_____Eastern Star
- (8)_____Odd Fellows
- (9)_____Rebeccas
- (0)_____Lions

69
- (1)_____Moose
- (2)_____Eagles
- (3)_____Labor Union
- (4)_____Farm Bureau
- (5)_____Farm Union
- (6)_____Grange

69 (Cont.)
- (7)_____Chamber of Commerce or Community Business Club
- (8)_____Kiwanis
- (9)_____Shrine
- (0)_____Ladies' Aid

70
- (1)_____League of Womens Voters
- (2)_____Neighborhood or other social card playing group
- (3)_____Country club or golf club
- (4)_____Study or literary club
- (5)_____American Automobile Association (AAA)
- (6)_____A sportsman club
- (7)_____American Association of University Women
- (8)_____National origin group (such as Sons of Norway)
- (9)_____Church club or group
- (0)_____Athletic club or group
- (x)_____Hobby club or group
- (    ) Others_____

The following items are related to your attitudes, feelings, and experiences. Remember that all of the information on this questionnaire is treated as confidential. Circle T if the item is true for you and F if it is false.

21. T F I meet strangers easily.

22. T F I get along as well as the average person in social activities.

23. T F In school I sometimes have been sent to the principal for cutting up.

24. T F I feel self-conscious when reciting in class.

25. T F I am sure I get a raw deal from life.

26. T F I feel at ease with people.

27. · T F At times I have very much wanted to leave home.

28. T F I have difficulty in starting a conversation with a person who has just been introduced.

29. T F I find it hard to keep my mind on a task or job.

30. T F I enjoy speaking before groups of people.

31. T F I know who is responsible for most of my troubles.

32. · T F My parents have often objected to the kind of people I go around with.

33. T F I am rather shy in contacts with people.

34. T F No one seems to understand me.

35. T F I enjoy entertaining people.

36. T F My family does not like the work I have chosen or the work I intend to choose for my life work.

37. T F I like to meet new people.

38. T F My parents and family find more fault with me than they should.

39. T F I dislike social affairs.

40. T F If people had not had it in for me I would have been much more successful.

41. T F I find it easy to express my ideas.

42. T F I wish I were not so shy.

43. T F I avoid people when it is possible.

44. T F I have had very peculiar and strange experiences.

45. T F I stay in the background at parties or social gatherings.

46. T F Most of my close friends are planning to go to college.

47. Would you say that your high school grades are a fairly accurate reflection of your ability?

　　1_____Yes 2_____No

48. Do you think that most of the important things that happen to people are: (Check one)

(1)_____More the result of circumstances beyond their control.

(2)_____More the result of their own efforts.

49. If you had your choice, which type of job would you pick? (Check one)

(1)_____A job which pays quite a low income but which you are sure of keeping.

(2)_____A job which pays a good income but which you have a 50-50 chance of losing.

(3)_____A job which pays an extremely good income if you make the grade but in which you lose almost everything if you don't make it.

(224-4)

12

isters the Minnesota Statewide Testing Program in which the Minnesota Scholastic Aptitude Test is taken by students in their junior year of high school and high school achievement data are collected at the end of the junior year.

The Minnesota Scholastic Aptitude Test (MSAT) provides a single score predictive of success in Minnesota colleges. The test is a shortened, time-limited form of the Ohio Psychological Examination, Form 26 (Berdie, Layton, Swanson, *et al.*, 1962).

The high school percentile rank is computed from the achievement data supplied by the high school and is based on all grades earned by the student during his freshman, sophomore, and junior years or his sophomore and junior years, depending upon whether he was in a three- or four-year high school. The rank shows the relative standing of the student in his class. A percentile rank of 100 places him within the top 1 percent; a percentile rank of 1 places him within the bottom 1 percent; a percentile rank of 64 indicates that 64 percent of the students obtained grade-point averages equal to or less than his. The high school percentile rank is one of the best indicators of academic success in college. Whereas the Minnesota Scholastic Aptitude Test tends to predict grades as well as would be indicated by a correlation coefficient of .45 to .55, the high school percentile rank yields a correlation coefficient of .50 to .60. A measure combining high school percentile rank and Minnesota Scholastic Aptitude Test score predicts as well as would be indicated by a correlation coefficient between .55 and .65.

Each biennium, or oftener when significant changes are made in the program, the Student Counseling Bureau conducts a "Survey of Scholastic Aptitude in Minnesota Colleges" for the Association of Minnesota Colleges. Each college furnishes a list of its entering freshmen to the Student Counseling Bureau, which finds the high school percentile rank and the scholastic aptitude score for each student. Summary reports are then published showing means and standard deviations for these variables by sex, by college, by type of college, and for the total group. In 1962, in addition to the names of entering freshmen, all Minnesota colleges furnished the Counseling Bureau with first-year grade-point averages for their freshmen in 1961–62.

In this study the achievement criterion used for college work was the grade-point average for the entire freshman year. For those students who dropped out of college without completing their freshman year, the grade-point average of the one semester or the one or two quarters during which the student was enrolled was used. Students who had not completed at least one quarter or semester were not included.

## Sample of Students

Of the 46,000 seniors graduating from Minnesota high schools in 1961, approximately 18,000, or 41 percent, attended college the following September. Among the college-bound students, approximately 15,000 attended college in Minnesota. For this group of 15,000 freshmen, an attempt was made to locate each student's questionnaire data, his test score, and the grades he received in whatever college he attended. For certain of the students, some of these data were missing. Others attended college for only a short period in the fall and dropped out before obtaining any grades. A small group was excluded from the study because typographical errors or similarity of names (the many Robert Johnsons and John Andersons, for instance) made it impossible to match data for them with any degree of certainty. The three types of information were found and matched for 12,405 students — 6,959 boys and 5,446 girls. The number in each of the different types of colleges in the state is shown in Table 1.

Table 1. Number of Minnesota Freshmen in Each Type of College

| Type of College | Men | Women |
|---|---|---|
| University of Minnesota | 3,145 | 2,065 |
| Private liberal arts colleges (8) | 827 | 901 |
| Catholic men's colleges (3) | 657 | |
| Catholic women's colleges (4) | | 541 |
| State colleges (5) | 1,473 | 1,344 |
| Junior colleges (11) | 857 | 595 |
| Total number of freshmen | 6,959 | 5,446 |

## Sample of Colleges

All regionally accredited four-year colleges and all public junior colleges in Minnesota cooperated in this study. Included were the eight private liberal arts colleges in the state, the three Catholic men's colleges (liberal arts), the four Catholic women's colleges (liberal arts), the five public state colleges, the ten public junior colleges, the one private junior college, and seven colleges of the University of Minnesota (two on campuses outside the Twin Cities). All the colleges of the university which admit any substantial number of freshman students were included; but several small departments, which admit only a few students to nondegree programs, such as dental hygiene and X-ray technology, were omitted. The only institutions of higher education in the state which were not covered in this study were several small nonaccredited Bible colleges and several religious seminaries. In all, 38 colleges were included — 31 separate institutions plus 7 colleges of the University of Minnesota.

## Analysis of Data

In a few cases the entire population of college freshmen was examined as one group. In most cases, however, this population was divided by sex and according to type of college attended. Each of the units of the university was analyzed separately. The private Protestant coeducational liberal arts colleges were usually examined as a group. The three Catholic men's colleges were treated as a group as were the four Catholic women's colleges. The eleven junior colleges were sometimes treated as one group and sometimes divided into "range junior colleges" and "other junior colleges" with the private junior college excluded. The "range junior colleges" are all located on Minnesota's iron range and a large proportion of the parents of the students who enter these colleges are or were employed in the iron mining industry. The "other junior colleges" are located in small cities in the state, most of them in fairly prosperous farming areas. The five state colleges, formerly state teachers colleges but now offering more diverse curricula, were also usually examined as a group.

In the initial analysis, differences among the colleges and the types of colleges were explored by computing distributions, means, and percentages for each of the different ability, socioeconomic, and personality variables. After these differences had been noted, the extent to which each of these variables was related to achievement in college was found. Then, multiple regression analysis was used to determine which of the variables were related to achievement in the different types of colleges after ability and previous achievement record had been taken into account. This type of analysis also yielded the maximum variance in the prediction of college achievement when all these variables — ability, achievement, socioeconomic background, cultural status of home, and certain personality characteristics — were taken into account.

Particular groups of college-entering freshmen, such as those from farms, those from lower socioeconomic groups, those of particular levels of ability, and those with certain personality characteristics, were studied as separate samples. The achievement of these groups in each of the different types of colleges was studied.

Certain of the statistical analyses in this study made use of regression equations or data taken from computer programs which included regression equations. In such analyses, complete data must be available for the entire sample. Therefore, if a student left unanswered any of the questionnaire items being studied, he could not be included in that portion of the analysis. In certain parts of the study then, the numbers are considerably reduced from those shown in Table 1.

## Chapter 3

# ACADEMIC ACHIEVEMENT LEVELS IN
# DIFFERENT COLLEGES

LARGE DIFFERENCES in the ability levels of student populations characterize American colleges. An examination of the scores achieved on any scholastic aptitude test or records of high school achievement for students in several different types of institutions shows this clearly. College Board scores, for example, have a mean of 500 and a standard deviation of 100 for a certain large group of college-bound young people. One college may have a mean College Board verbal score of 650 for its freshman class with no students scoring below 500 and at another college the mean verbal score may be 260 with no student scoring above 480. In this extreme example, the ablest student at one college attains a score below that of the least able student at another college.

Where a high school student's score falls in the distribution of scores in the population at a particular college is strongly related to whether or not he will be admitted to that college. Furthermore, after admission a student's academic success at college is related to how his various abilities compare with the distribution of ability levels of the rest of the student body at his institution. High school counselors have long recognized these differences and have usually tried to make some estimate of the range of abilities of students in various colleges in helping their students select which colleges they will apply to. Recent publications such as the *Manual of Freshman Class Profiles*, published by the College Entrance Examination Board (1964), have given counselors objective information to use so they need not rely on educated guesses.

Such differences exist among the colleges in Minnesota and in studying the academic achievement of students in different colleges it is necessary to control the differences in the levels of ability among the freshman classes in these colleges. In beginning to make such comparisons in this study, however, a further problem arose which had not been expected. Even when ability and previous achievement were controlled, not only did certain types of students obtain different levels of academic achievement in different colleges but *all* students in particular colleges achieved different levels from those achieved by similar types of students at other colleges. An important factor which was not being controlled was the difference in the grading distributions of various colleges. *Our data showed clearly that the grade-point average achieved by a student in a given college is greatly affected by the over-all distribution of grades in that college.* The purposes of this chapter are (1) to examine these differences in grading distributions, (2) to show their effect on the grades achieved by students in different colleges, and (3) to describe a method by which student achievement levels in various colleges may be compared.

## Comparing Ability and Grading Distributions in Different Colleges

The information shown in Table 2 provides evidence that large differences in ability levels and grading distributions do exist among the various colleges in Minnesota. On a distribution of scholastic aptitude test scores for all college-bound students in the state, the mean score for one college falls at the 17th percentile while another falls at the 97th percentile.

Table 2. Percentile of Mean Freshman Minnesota Scholastic Aptitude Test Scores and Mean Freshman Year Grade-Point Averages in Different Types of Minnesota Colleges

| Type of College | No. of Colleges | No. of Freshmen | MSAT Mean Raw Score | | First-Year GPA | | |
|---|---|---|---|---|---|---|---|
| | | | Percentile [a] of Mean MSAT Scores | Percentile [a] Range of Mean MSAT Scores | Mean | SD | Range |
| University of Minnesota | | | | | | | |
| College of Agriculture .... | 1 | 383 | 50.5 | | 2.0 | .77 | |
| Institute of Technology ... | 1 | 627 | 71.5 | | 2.0 | .83 | |
| General College .......... | 1 | 795 | 17.6 | | 1.8 | .68 | |
| College of Liberal Arts .... | 1 | 2,422 | 67.1 | | 2.0 | .80 | |
| Private liberal arts colleges .. | 8 | 1,727 | 69.1 | 62–97 | 2.3 | .71 | 2.0–2.6 |
| Catholic men's colleges ..... | 3 | 656 | 61.0 | 57–66 | 2.1 | .79 | 1.9–2.4 |
| Catholic women's colleges .... | 4 | 541 | 68.3 | 65–72 | 2.6 | .62 | 2.5–2.8 |
| State colleges .............. | 5 | 2,816 | 38.6 | 33–52 | 2.0 | .75 | 1.9–2.2 |
| Junior colleges ............. | 11 | 1,355 | 43.7 | 35–92 | 2.1 | .74 | 1.9–2.3 |

[a] Based on Minnesota all-college freshmen norms.

The information given in this table, as is true of the rest of the tables in the book, is for Minnesota students who attended Minnesota colleges. For certain of the state colleges, these figures include almost all the entering freshmen, while for others, particularly a few of the private liberal arts colleges, Minnesota students represent a much smaller proportion of their freshman classes. Grades reported here are on a four-point system: A = 4, B = 3, C = 2, D = 1, and F = 0. In the case of the three colleges in Minnesota which, in 1961–62, graded on a three-point system, course grades were obtained and recalculated on a four-point system.

As Table 2 shows, among colleges of some types, for example the eight private liberal arts colleges, mean ability levels vary considerably. For certain other types, however, such as the state colleges, mean ability levels of entering freshman classes are similar. The figures shown here for Minnesota are probably fairly close to those from many states. An exception might be the situation among the private colleges. Minnesota does not have any small private liberal arts colleges that must struggle to obtain a freshman class of adequate size; the ones in this study can be somewhat selective. Therefore, the range of mean ability levels among the private colleges may be more restricted than would be found in some states.

The mean grade-point averages shown in Table 2 indicate that the range among the colleges is from 1.8 to 2.8. *There was little relationship between the ability of students in a particular college and mean grade-point average received at that college.* The students in the university's College of Liberal Arts and Institute of Technology rank among the top of the college groups on ability but near the bottom on mean grade-point average. The average student in a state college receives exactly the same grade as does the student in the university's College of Liberal Arts, although the average student in the College of Liberal Arts has considerably greater ability than the average student in a state college. The average girl in the university's College of Liberal Arts received a 2.1 average while the average girl in a Catholic women's college with a slightly lower average test score received a 2.6 average.

Even among colleges of a particular type such as the private liberal arts colleges, there was still a considerable range in both the mean grade-point averages and the mean aptitude test scores and there was little relationship between the ability of students in the particular liberal arts college and the mean grade-point average they received. For example, at two private liberal arts colleges, one falling third highest among the colleges in Minnesota in mean scholastic aptitude test score and one falling slightly below the state median of individual college means, the mean freshman grade-point average was the same — 2.4.

The variance or shape of the distribution of grade-point averages about the mean was similar in almost all colleges. (In the typical college the standard deviation was .7.) Since 2.0 is a passing grade-point average (for graduation) in all colleges, the difference in mean grade-point average between 2.0 and 2.3 can be an important one. At a school where the mean grade-point average is 2.3, less than a third of the freshmen will receive below-passing averages as compared with half of the students at a college where the mean grade-point average is 2.0.

## The Effect of Differing Grade Distributions on Students in Different Colleges

An example of the effect that varying levels of competition and varying grading practices can have upon the grades of reasonably able stu-

Table 3. Percentage of High-Ability [a] Students Receiving Below-Passing Grade-Point Averages at Different Types of Minnesota Colleges

| Type of College | No. of Students | No. with MSAT above 45 | Percentage of High-Ability Students with GPA below 2.00 | |
|---|---|---|---|---|
| | | | Mean | Range |
| *Men* | | | | |
| University of Minnesota | | | | |
| College of Agriculture ......... | 231 | 55 | 40 | |
| Institute of Technology ........ | 617 | 338 | 39 | |
| College of Liberal Arts ........ | 666 | 280 | 35 | |
| Private liberal arts colleges ...... | 327 | 422 | 26 | 5–36 |
| Catholic men's colleges .......... | 656 | 258 | 27 | 14–37 |
| State colleges ................... | 1,472 | 196 | 26 | 14–37 |
| Junior colleges ................. | 811 | 149 | 28 | 10–43 |
| *Women* | | | | |
| University of Minnesota | | | | |
| College of Agriculture ......... | 152 | 55 | 13 | |
| Institute of Technology ........ | 10 | 9 | 11 | |
| College of Liberal Arts ........ | 1,120 | 524 | 20 | |
| Private liberal arts colleges ...... | 900 | 495 | 11 | 3–15 |
| Catholic women's colleges ........ | 541 | 276 | 6 | 0–10 |
| State colleges ................... | 1,344 | 341 | 11 | 4–14 |
| Junior colleges ................. | 544 | 158 | 13 | 0–31 |

[a] High ability is defined as having an MSAT raw score of 45 or above. This places the student in the upper one-fifth of high school graduates and the upper one-third of college freshmen in Minnesota.

dents is seen in Table 3. These students received scholastic aptitude test scores which placed them in the top one-fifth of the high school graduates of the state and among the top third of the college freshmen in the state. At one Catholic men's college, for example, 37 percent of such able freshmen received less than C averages as compared with 14 percent at another. Forty percent of the high-ability men received below-passing grades at the colleges of the university as compared with approximately 25 percent at other colleges. Less attention should be paid to the range of percentages at the state and junior colleges since certain of these colleges enrolled only small numbers of such high-ability students.

A look at the proportions of students who had high school records which placed them in the top 15 percent of their high school graduating class but who received less than a 2.0 in college revealed similar differences (Table 4). At the University of Minnesota, 25 percent of the men in the College of Liberal Arts and 31 percent in the Institute of Technology with high achievement records in high school received less-than-passing grades. Of such men in the private liberal arts and Catholic col-

Table 4. Percentage of High-Achieving* Students Receiving Below-Passing Grade-Point Averages at Different Types of Minnesota Colleges

| Type of College | No. of Students | No. with HSR above 85 | Percentage of High-Ability Students with GPA below 2.00 | |
|---|---|---|---|---|
| | | | Mean | Range |
| *Men* | | | | |
| University of Minnesota | | | | |
|    College of Agriculture ......... | 231 | 46 | 13 | |
|    Institute of Technology ........ | 617 | 326 | 31 | |
|    College of Liberal Arts ........ | 666 | 218 | 25 | |
| Private liberal arts colleges ...... | 826 | 325 | 13 | 6–18 |
| Catholic men's colleges .......... | 657 | 181 | 13 | 8–18 |
| State colleges .................. | 1,473 | 152 | 9 | 0–15 |
| Junior colleges .................. | 861 | 124 | 7 | 0–21 |
| *Women* | | | | |
| University of Minnesota | | | | |
|    College of Agriculture ......... | 152 | 577 | 12 | |
|    Institute of Technology ........ | 10 | 10 | 20 | |
|    College of Liberal Arts ......... | 1,108 | 518 | 18 | |
| Private liberal arts colleges ...... | 901 | 523 | 9 | 3–15 |
| Catholic women's colleges ........ | 534 | 222 | 1 | 0–4 |
| State colleges .................. | 1,341 | 397 | 6 | 0–9 |
| Junior colleges .................. | 606 | 178 | 4 | 0–13 |

* Graduated among the top 15 percent of their high school class.

leges, 13 percent had below a 2.0; for junior colleges this proportion was 7 percent. Eighteen percent of the girls in the top 15 percent of their high school class obtained less than 2.0 averages at the College of Liberal Arts, as compared with only 1 percent of the girls who attended Catholic women's colleges.

Another method of examining these differences is to take a student at a particular ability level and compute the grade-point average he would typically receive at a number of different colleges. This can be accomplished by computing the means and standard deviations of both scholastic aptitude test scores and grade-point averages at each of the different types of colleges. It is then possible to take a student with a certain score and determine where he would fall on the distribution in a particular type of college. By taking the same point on the distribution of freshman grade-point averages for each type of college, the grades a student at a certain level of ability might achieve at each type of institution can be compared. This procedure makes the assumption that a perfect relationship or correlation exists between test scores and grades, and this is certainly not the case. This approach does show, however, the way in which differences in grading practices and levels of competition affect students at particular ability levels at various colleges.

A student who falls at the 75th percentile for college-bound students on a scholastic aptitude test would be brighter than three out of four freshmen who attend college in Minnesota. In the university's Institute of Technology or College of Liberal Arts he would receive a just-passing C average (Table 5). At a private liberal arts college in the state he would typically earn a C+ or 2.4 average and in a state or junior college

Table 5. Freshman Grade-Point Averages Which Would Typically Be Obtained by Students of Various Ability Levels [a] at Different Types of Minnesota Colleges

| Type of College | 50th Percentile | 75th Percentile | 90th Percentile | 95th Percentile |
|---|---|---|---|---|
| University of Minnesota | | | | |
| College of Agriculture | 2.09 | 2.65 | 3.15 | 3.45 |
| Institute of Technology | 1.45 | 2.07 | 2.64 | 2.97 |
| College of Liberal Arts | 1.64 | 2.25 | 2.80 | 3.13 |
| Private liberal arts colleges | 1.91 | 2.43 | 2.89 | 3.17 |
| Catholic men's colleges | 1.87 | 2.47 | 3.00 | 3.32 |
| Catholic women's colleges | 2.25 | 2.69 | 3.09 | 3.33 |
| State colleges | 2.34 | 2.91 | 3.43 | 3.62 |
| Junior colleges | 2.31 | 2.84 | 3.32 | 3.74 |

[a] As measured by MSAT percentile rank among all college-bound students.

receive a B— or about a 2.8 average. If he were at the 50th percentile (of average ability for college-bound students) he would be expected to flunk out of the university's Institute of Technology or College of Liberal Arts with a 1.4 to 1.6 average. He would be placed on probation at the typical liberal arts college or Catholic men's college but would receive a solid C average at a Catholic women's college, a junior college, or a state college.

## Computing a "Difficulty Index"

In order to take a further look at the differences in levels of achievement attained by students at different colleges, a more sophisticated method of examining the differences was devised. This technique resulted in the computation of a "difficulty index" for each college in the state. This index was computed as follows: The means and standard deviations for the statewide population of students entering college were computed for high school rank, MSAT score, and freshman grade-point average. The mean was also computed for each of the individual colleges in the state on each of these three variables. The distance each of these colleges fell above or below that for the over-all college mean was measured in terms of a z score computed according to the following formula:

$$z = \frac{\text{college mean} - \text{mean for all colleges}}{\text{standard deviation for all colleges}}$$

A college whose entering freshmen had a mean MSAT score falling half a standard deviation above the mean for the statewide population of entering freshmen would receive a z score on the MSAT variable of +.5. A college with a mean grade-point average a quarter of a standard deviation below the mean grade-point average earned by all freshmen in all colleges would receive a z score on grade-point average of −.25.

A college whose entering freshman class obtained a mean scholastic aptitude test score which fell well above the statewide mean but a mean freshman grade-point average which fell at the mean would be an institution where it would be more difficult than at most other colleges for a particular student to earn a high grade-point average. A student attending a college with an entering freshman class whose ability fell below the statewide mean but whose mean grade-point average fell above the statewide mean would find it easier to obtain a high grade-point average than if he had entered a college closer to the "typical" one in Minnesota. The $z$ score of the ability variable was therefore subtracted from the $z$ score of the mean grade-point average for each college. Colleges with minus $z$ score differences were more difficult institutions than colleges with positive $z$ score differences. Differences in $z$ scores were computed both for high school rank and for scholastic aptitude test score for each college. Since the pattern of achievement varies between the sexes, these differences were originally obtained separately for each sex but were combined for the purposes of this study.

In a regression equation utilizing high school rank and MSAT to predict college grades, there was a considerable range among the colleges in the different weights given to each of the variables (HSR:MSAT ranged from 1:1 to 12:1). In the typical college, high school rank received a weight approximately twice that for MSAT score; therefore, in combining these two variables to obtain a single $z$ score difference for each college, the differences for each of these variables were combined in a 2:1 ratio. The resulting single $z$ score was then used as a difficulty index for each of the colleges. The difficulty indexes (differences between $z$ scores on mean grade-point average and mean ability) are shown for each of the colleges in Minnesota in Table 6. Since the shapes of the distribution of grades and, therefore, the standard deviations were quite similar in all the colleges, the difficulty index was converted into a rough estimate of actual difference on grade-point average by multiplying the index by the standard deviation of grade-point averages for all colleges. These estimates for differences on grade-point averages also appear in Table 6. The items in this column should be read in this way: A student who attends the university's Institute of Technology should expect to receive a grade-point average .66 of a grade point below that which he would receive in the "average" college. There is a difference of over a full grade point (1.32) between the college at the top of the list and that at the bottom. This is the difference between a failing grade of less than 2.0 and an honors grade of above 3.0.

The information shown in Table 6 indicates that the university's Institute of Technology and College of Liberal Arts and several of the private liberal arts colleges have the brightest students and give the lowest grades. At the bottom of the list is the university's General College, a junior college that takes students who are not admissible to other colleges within the university. (General College students achieving grades in the top third of their class are allowed to transfer to other colleges of the university.) The reason for the larger number of colleges

Table 6. Difficulty Indexes [a] and Estimates of Grade-Point Average Differences [b] among Freshman Classes at Various Minnesota Colleges [c]

| College | Difficulty Index | Estimated GPA Differences from All Colleges (Mean of 2.03) |
|---|---|---|
| UM Institute of Technology | −.87 | −.66 |
| Private liberal arts college F | −.63 | −.48 |
| UM College of Liberal Arts | −.40 | −.30 |
| Private liberal arts college B | −.39 | −.30 |
| Private liberal arts college H | −.30 | −.23 |
| Private liberal arts college G | −.29 | −.22 |
| Private liberal arts college A | −.26 | −.20 |
| UM College of Education | −.21 | −.16 |
| UM Morris | −.17 | −.13 |
| Private liberal arts college E | −.14 | −.11 |
| Private liberal arts college C | −.09 | −.07 |
| Catholic men's college B | −.07 | −.05 |
| UM College of Agriculture | −.05 | −.04 |
| UM Duluth | +.01 | +.01 |
| Catholic men's college A | +.02 | +.02 |
| Junior college D | +.03 | +.02 |
| Catholic men's college C | +.10 | +.08 |
| Private liberal arts college D | +.11 | +.08 |
| State college E | +.13 | +.10 |
| State college A | +.14 | +.11 |
| Junior college H | +.14 | +.11 |
| Catholic women's college C | +.16 | +.12 |
| Range junior college E | +.17 | +.13 |
| Catholic women's college D | +.21 | +.16 |
| Catholic women's college B | +.27 | +.21 |
| Range junior college G | +.32 | +.24 |
| State college B | +.38 | +.29 |
| State college C | +.38 | +.29 |
| Private junior college I | +.40 | +.30 |
| Range junior college A | +.40 | +.30 |
| Range junior college C | +.48 | +.36 |
| Junior college J | +.49 | +.37 |
| Junior college B | +.51 | +.39 |
| Junior college K | +.53 | +.40 |
| Range junior college F | +.56 | +.43 |
| Catholic women's college A | +.58 | +.44 |
| State college D | +.58 | +.44 |
| UM General College | +.87 | +.66 |

[a] Differences between z scores for grade-point averages and for mean ability (weighted HSR:MSAT, 2:1).

[b] Estimated grade-point average = difficulty index × standard deviation of grade-point averages for all freshmen.

[c] For all freshmen: mean HSR = 67.15 (SD = 24.24); mean MSAT = 39.2, or 54th percentile (SD = 13.8); mean GPA = 2.03 (SD = .76).

with positive z scores is that several of those with negative scores, such as the university's College of Liberal Arts and the Institute of Technology, include large numbers of freshmen, thereby offsetting many smaller schools. The colleges with positive z scores are a general mixture of state colleges, Catholic women's colleges, and junior colleges, without any particular groupings among these three types.

An obvious question is to what extent are the figures shown here for Minnesota colleges representative of similar types of institutions elsewhere? Colleges of engineering in large universities throughout the country are notorious for their policy of giving low grades to able students. Engineering colleges fail more able students than any other type of institution. Therefore the fact that the University of Minnesota's Institute of Technology shows up here as the one with the highest difficulty index in the state is not at all surprising. Several other colleges at the University of Minnesota have fairly able entering freshman classes but give very low grade distributions, averaging approximately 2.0. Such a mean grade-point average is low for colleges which are selective and is also well below the mean grade-point averages of other Big Ten institutions. (The grade-point averages shown here for the University of Minnesota have remained constant over a long period of years.) The mean grade-point average for the typical private college in the country is similar to Minnesota's colleges, in the general range of 2.3 to 2.6. Junior colleges and state colleges which admit any student with a high school diploma probably tend to run somewhat below this, in the general vicinity of 2.0 to 2.2. In this study Catholic women's colleges tended to have a high grading curve. It is not known whether this is typical only of Minnesota or only of Catholic women's colleges, or whether it is the typical pattern for smaller women's colleges of all types.

Many students from various colleges in Minnesota transfer each year to the University of Minnesota, in particular to its College of Liberal Arts. It was therefore possible to compare students' previous grade-point averages with those achieved after transferring to the university. All students who transferred from other Minnesota colleges to the university's College of Liberal Arts in 1963 were followed up by the university's Admissions Office. The differences in grade-point averages before and after transfer were compared with those predicted from the difficulty indexes. Table 6 suggests that students transferring from state college B, which has an estimated GPA difference of +.29, to the university's College of Liberal Arts, with an estimated difference of −.30, would typically drop .59 in their grade-point average. The actual decrease in grade-point average by these students, as shown in Table 7, was .53. (In this table the grade-point averages for work at a previous college are based on all the work completed there — a maximum of two years' work, most often approximately one year, since these students were transferring into the Lower Division of the College of Liberal Arts.

Table 7. Comparisons between Predicted and Actual Differences in Grade-Point Average for Students Transferring from Minnesota Colleges to the University of Minnesota College of Liberal Arts, Lower Division, 1963–64

| College | No. of Students Transferring [a] | GPA Previous College | UM CLA | Predicted Difference | Actual Difference |
|---|---|---|---|---|---|
| All state colleges ............. | 134 | 2.41 | 1.89 | | −.52 |
| State college B ............. | 40–50 | 2.47 | 1.94 | −.59 | −.53 |
| State college A ............. | 40–50 | 2.29 | 1.83 | −.41 | −.46 |
| All junior colleges ............. | 57 | 2.52 | 2.09 | | −.43 |
| Junior college H ............. | 10–20 | 2.54 | 2.17 | −.41 | −.37 |
| Junior college D ............. | 10–20 | 2.49 | 1.94 | −.32 | −.55 |
| All private colleges ............ | 266 | 2.43 | 2.26 | | −.17 |
| Private liberal arts college G... | 20–40 | 2.59 | 2.51 | −.08 | −.08 |
| Private liberal arts college A .. | 20–40 | 2.65 | 2.52 | −.10 | −.13 |
| Catholic men's college A ...... | 20–40 | 2.46 | 1.67 | −.32 | −.79 |
| Catholic men's college B ...... | 20–40 | 2.17 | 2.13 | −.25 | −.04 |
| Catholic women's college B .... | 10–20 | 2.84 | 2.41 | −.51 | −.43 |
| All Minnesota colleges .......... | 457 | 2.44 | 2.14 | | −.30 |

[a] Approximate numbers are reported to conceal the identity of the colleges.

The grade-point average given for the College of Liberal Arts represents a full year of course work if by June of 1964 the student had completed a full year. If the grades for only one or two quarters in the College of Liberal Arts were available, then that grade-point average was used.) The 47 students who transferred from state college B received a mean grade-point average of 2.47 in that college; in the College of Liberal Arts at the university they received a 1.94 and so the predicted drop was very close to the actual difference. Similar data are given for other colleges in the remainder of Table 7. Within each type of college data for the one or two colleges with the largest number transferring to the University of Minnesota are shown. In the case of the junior colleges, the Catholic women's colleges, and one of the Catholic men's colleges, these numbers were small and therefore the mean grade-point average shown here cannot be considered very stable.

In most cases the actual differences in grade-point averages for transfer students were similar to the predicted differences. Only in the case of the two Catholic men's colleges shown do the actual differences in grade-point averages vary greatly from the predicted differences.

*The results shown here indicate that mean grade-point averages achieved by groups of students who transferred from one college to another can be accurately predicted from the "difficulty index" yielded by the procedure described above.* The accuracy of these predictions could not have been obtained by making use of differences of level in competition alone. Differences in grading distributions must also be taken into account.

The data in Table 7 also clearly show that students transferring from most other colleges to the state university experience a drop in grade-point average. Similar results have been reported for transfers from junior colleges by Hills (1964) and by Knoell and Medsker (1965). Different environment, larger classes, and changes in teaching methods are explanations which have been advanced to explain the lower grade-point averages achieved by junior college students when they transfer to state universities. However, the results of the study reported here have clearly established that the chief cause of "transfer shock," as this phenomenon has been labeled, is the higher level of competition at the state university, which is not accompanied by a higher distribution of grades. These results also show that the amount of "transfer shock" experienced by transferring students varies considerably according to which state or junior colleges they come from.

It could be argued that the students earn the grades they receive and that the differences presented here are actually due to the fact that students in a college with an average ability level but an above average mean grade point have actually learned more, as indicated by their higher grades. The data on transfer students tend to refute such an argument. Certain colleges whose students achieve fairly high grades at the state university may attribute this to better preparation at their college, smaller classes, better teaching methods, a better environment for learning, or a more favorable intellectual climate. There is little evidence from this study to show that any of these factors are at all important. The achievement of transfer students can be accurately predicted by considering only ability levels and grading distributions. The differences in grading distributions and the lack of their relationship to student ability levels as revealed here highlight a major problem within the higher education establishment in this country. Differences in grading practices among various departments on an individual campus are every bit as large as the differences among institutions.

Colleges in this country should examine their grading practices to see how they compare with other institutions. Particular attention should be given to those colleges where the student body has changed as that institution has become more selective. The type of differences in levels of achievement shown here can be crucial not only to students who transfer but also those who apply for admission or for financial aid in professional and graduate training programs. School counselors should consider not only levels of competition but also distributions of grade-point averages as they help their students with the problem of college selection.

Chapter 4

# SOCIOECONOMIC FACTORS AND COLLEGE CHOICE

STUDENTS ATTEMPTING to decide which college to attend sometimes ask whether or not they will find at a particular college many students with attitudes, values, and backgrounds like their own. The able girl from a lower-class background who wins a scholarship to an expensive private college may choose to go elsewhere because of her feeling that she will not "fit in." A wealthy boy may refuse to even consider the local junior college for the same reason. Some students have little choice. With few exceptions, the boy who wishes to study engineering or agriculture must attend a large public university. A girl who wishes to attend an all-girls' school must choose a small private college. In the same way a Jewish student in the Midwest seeking a nearby college with a sizable group of Jewish classmates is pretty much limited to the larger public universities.

Considerable information about the socioeconomic and cultural backgrounds of the students who attended the various colleges in Minnesota was available for this study, and the way they differed among these colleges was examined. Also the relationships between these factors and college achievement was studied.

## Occupation of Father

One of the best indices of socioeconomic background is the occupational level of the father. On the high school questionnaire the students were asked to check one of seven categories describing their father's occupation: (1) profession, (2) owns or manages business, (3) office work, (4) sales, (5) owns or manages farm, (6) skilled tradesman, or (7) factory worker. In the cases where they could not readily classify their father's occupation, they were asked to check "other" and to write in the name of the "other" occupation. Where possible, coders classified this

30

occupation into one of the seven categories; otherwise it was left in a miscellaneous group.

The proportions of students who reported their fathers in each of the different occupational classifications are shown for each type of college in Table 8. *The information shown here clearly indicates that the more expensive private colleges do not attract exclusively students from professional or managerial homes, nor are the student populations in the junior colleges made up primarily of students from lower socioeconomic levels.* Colleges do differ in the family occupational levels of their students but these differences are not as great as might be expected. Private liberal arts colleges have more students from professional homes than do state or junior colleges, and the junior colleges have more students whose fathers are skilled tradesmen or unskilled laborers than do private liberal arts colleges. Even so, substantial proportions of students from both types of backgrounds are found in both types of colleges. Even the most expensive colleges apparently have enough scholarships and aid available to attract some students from lower socioeconomic backgrounds.

In Table 8 it may also be seen that the university's College of Agriculture does not attract primarily students from agricultural backgrounds — only one-third are from farms (approximately one-half of the boys and one-quarter of the girls).

Engineering presumably attracts more students from lower socioeconomic backgrounds than liberal arts programs since large numbers of engineering students are supposed to come from families of skilled tradesmen. When the percentage of students from lower socioeconomic backgrounds who were enrolled in the university's Institute of Technology is compared with the percentage in its College of Liberal Arts, this supposition is not confirmed. The proportions in both colleges coming from either a skilled trade background or a laboring background were essentially the same. In Minnesota, then, this assumption does not hold now although such differences may very well have been the case in years past. Engineering schools now require considerable amounts of mathematics and science in high school and their curricula have increasingly emphasized theoretical over applied course work. These academic changes as well as possible shifts in the image or stereotype of the engineering profession may have caused students from different backgrounds to be attracted to these fields.

The proportions of students from all types of backgrounds were essentially the same in both the Institute of Technology and the College

Table 8. Percentage of Freshmen at Different Types of Minnesota Colleges by Occupation of Students' Fathers

| Type of College | No. of Freshmen | Professional | Owns or Manages Business | Office Worker | Sales | Owns or Manages Farm | Skilled Tradesman | Factory Worker | Other |
|---|---|---|---|---|---|---|---|---|---|
| University of Minnesota | | | | | | | | | |
| College of Agriculture | 378 | 9% | 12% | 6% | 6% | 36% | 14% | 7% | 11% |
| Institute of Technology | 614 | 13 | 16 | 8 | 8 | 12 | 22 | 10 | 11 |
| College of Liberal Arts | 2,381 | 15 | 19 | 10 | 11 | 5 | 21 | 8 | 12 |
| Private liberal arts colleges | 1,715 | 20 | 18 | 7 | 8 | 16 | 13 | 6 | 12 |
| Catholic men's colleges | 647 | 14 | 22 | 11 | 9 | 9 | 16 | 9 | 10 |
| Catholic women's colleges | 524 | 12 | 22 | 7 | 10 | 12 | 16 | 8 | 13 |
| State colleges | 2,770 | 7 | 18 | 4 | 7 | 22 | 17 | 10 | 14 |
| Junior colleges | 1,432 | 5 | 12 | 5 | 4 | 13 | 23 | 24 | 14 |

of Liberal Arts with the exception of the smaller proportion of farm students in the College of Liberal Arts. This proportion was smaller, in fact, than that in any other type of college. Apparently when students of both sexes from farms decide to enter programs in liberal arts, they are far more likely to attend smaller colleges, either public or private, than they are to attend the large metropolitan University of Minnesota.

The junior colleges attract a higher proportion of students from unskilled and semiskilled laborer families than the other types of colleges. The principal reason for this is that over half of the junior colleges are located in cities on Minnesota's iron range. A substantial proportion of the students in these junior colleges come from families where the father is or was a worker in the iron mines.

One important point needs to be made about junior college students. The average socioeconomic level of junior college students is slightly below that of other colleges, but the junior colleges still attract students from the entire range of socioeconomic backgrounds including a number of students from professional and managerial homes. The ability levels of students in different colleges outlined in the previous chapter showed a similar pattern. While the mean ability level of students attending junior colleges is below that of most other types of colleges, junior colleges still attract students at all levels of ability including a number at the upper end of the distribution. In a recent investigation (Smith, 1966), Iowa students choosing two- and four-year colleges were compared on both ability level and parental occupational level. The results of this study were striking. Students from lower socioeconomic backgrounds at all levels of ability were quite likely to attend junior colleges. Among students from professional backgrounds, it was mainly those at the lower-ability levels who attended junior colleges. Students from professional backgrounds were likely to attend junior colleges only if their high school achievement record placed them in the lower half of their class. Almost no students of either sex who were in the top quintile in their high school class and who came from professional homes had any plans to enter a junior college. *In junior colleges, high-ability students almost always come from lower socioeconomic backgrounds while lower-ability students come from all socioeconomic levels.*

## Parental Education

On the high school questionnaire the students were asked to check the highest educational level achieved by each of their parents. The proportions of students checking each of the educational levels reached by their fathers are shown in Table 9. *All types of colleges have both substantial proportions of students whose fathers have completed no more than an eighth-grade education and substantial proportions whose fathers have had some college training.* These figures show that in the liberal arts colleges in the state, whether at the university, private liberal arts colleges, or Catholic liberal arts colleges, approximately 20 percent of the students come from homes where the father had no more than an eighth-grade education and approximately one-third came from homes in which the father had been to college. In the state and junior colleges approximately one-third of the students had fathers with no more than an eighth-grade education and approximately one-fifth of their fathers had completed some college.

Although the occupational levels of parents of students in the university's College of Liberal Arts resembled those of parents of Institute of Technology students, fathers of students in the College of Liberal Arts had reached slightly higher levels of education than fathers of students in engineering.

The comparison of different types of college by education of the students' mothers is shown in Table 10. *The differences among students in different colleges in the level of the mothers' education were smaller than the differences in fathers' education.* In other words, the different types of colleges varied more in fathers' educational level than in mothers'. For example, 38 percent of the students in the university's College of Liberal Arts had fathers with some college training as compared with 20 percent for students attending junior colleges — a difference of 18 percentage points. Of the mothers of students in the College of Liberal Arts, 30 percent had some college training compared with 24 percent of the mothers of students in the junior colleges — a difference of only 6 percentage points.

One exception to this pattern appears for the private liberal arts colleges where considerably more mothers had attended college than did mothers of students in any other type of college. *Apparently, if a student's mother has had some college training, the student is somewhat more likely to attend a smaller private liberal arts college than he is to attend other types of colleges including the university's College of Liberal Arts.* No similar relationship was found between fathers' education and matriculation at a small liberal arts college.

In general, the results of these analyses by occupation and education

Table 9. Percentage of Freshmen at Different Types of Minnesota Colleges by Education of Students' Fathers

| Type of College | No. of Freshmen | Some Grade School | Completed 8th Grade | Some High School | High School Graduate | Business or Trade School | Some College | College Graduate | More Than One College Degree |
|---|---|---|---|---|---|---|---|---|---|
| University of Minnesota | | | | | | | | | |
| College of Agriculture | 382 | 2% | 25% | 13% | 24% | 12% | 8% | 13% | 3% |
| Institute of Technology | 623 | 1 | 20 | 12 | 27 | 9 | 11 | 16 | 4 |
| College of Liberal Arts | 2,391 | 2 | 13 | 11 | 26 | 11 | 14 | 17 | 7 |
| Private liberal arts colleges | 1,720 | 2 | 17 | 9 | 22 | 11 | 13 | 16 | 10 |
| Catholic men's colleges | 654 | 2 | 16 | 10 | 27 | 8 | 14 | 17 | 6 |
| Catholic women's colleges | 529 | 4 | 20 | 10 | 24 | 10 | 13 | 13 | 7 |
| State colleges | 2,781 | 4 | 31 | 13 | 25 | 9 | 7 | 8 | 3 |
| Junior colleges | 1,444 | 4 | 28 | 16 | 25 | 7 | 9 | 9 | 2 |

Table 10. Percentage of Freshmen at Different Types of Minnesota Colleges by Education of Students' Mothers

| Type of College | No. of Freshmen | Some Grade School | Completed 8th Grade | Some High School | High School Graduate | Business or Trade School | Some College | College Graduate | More Than One College Degree |
|---|---|---|---|---|---|---|---|---|---|
| University of Minnesota | | | | | | | | | |
| College of Agriculture | 381 | 1% | 14% | 8% | 35% | 13% | 18% | 12% | 0% |
| Institute of Technology | 621 | 1 | 12 | 9 | 43 | 8 | 15 | 12 | 1 |
| College of Liberal Arts | 2,397 | 1 | 8 | 9 | 42 | 11 | 15 | 13 | 2 |
| Private liberal arts colleges | 1,726 | 0 | 9 | 6 | 29 | 13 | 21 | 20 | 2 |
| Catholic men's colleges | 651 | 1 | 11 | 9 | 38 | 8 | 16 | 14 | 2 |
| Catholic women's colleges | 538 | 2 | 13 | 9 | 32 | 13 | 18 | 13 | 1 |
| State colleges | 2,786 | 1 | 19 | 12 | 35 | 8 | 16 | 9 | 1 |
| Junior colleges | 1,447 | 2 | 15 | 15 | 39 | 6 | 12 | 11 | 1 |

testify to the great heterogeneity of backgrounds of students within each of the individual colleges. Both the selective, expensive, private colleges and the local, commuter, junior colleges have many students from unskilled, laboring backgrounds as well as many students from professional backgrounds. Variance within most American colleges exceeds the variance among colleges in the socioeconomic backgrounds from which their students are drawn.

## Family Help with College Expenses

The student questionnaire included an item on which students were asked to indicate the extent to which their families would help them pay their college expenses during the coming year. They checked whether their families could pay all, most, some, or none of their expenses. The proportions checking each of the categories are shown for each of the types of colleges in Table 11. As might be assumed, in all colleges girls expected that their families would contribute considerably more toward the cost of college than did boys. In each of the colleges 6–10 percent of the boys expected their parents to pay all their college expenses as compared with 15–20 percent of the girls. On the other hand,

Table 11. Percentage of Freshmen at Different Types of Minnesota Colleges by Reported Extent of Expected Family Help with College Expenses

| Type of College | No. of Freshmen | Expenses To Be Paid by Family | | | |
|---|---|---|---|---|---|
| | | All | Most | Some | None |
| *Men* | | | | | |
| University of Minnesota | | | | | |
| College of Agriculture ....... | 191 | 5% | 34% | 50% | 12% |
| Institute of Technology ....... | 594 | 6 | 25 | 53 | 17 |
| General College ............. | 427 | 9 | 27 | 48 | 16 |
| College of Liberal Arts ....... | 1,104 | 8 | 27 | 50 | 15 |
| Private liberal arts colleges ...... | 803 | 8 | 31 | 51 | 11 |
| Catholic men's colleges ......... | 625 | 9 | 28 | 49 | 14 |
| State colleges ................. | 1,180 | 6 | 29 | 50 | 14 |
| Junior colleges ................. | 736 | 8 | 32 | 46 | 14 |
| *Women* | | | | | |
| University of Minnesota | | | | | |
| College of Agriculture ........ | 135 | 13 | 37 | 41 | 8 |
| Institute of Technology ....... | 9 | 0 | 33 | 56 | 11 |
| General College ............. | 185 | 29 | 37 | 30 | 4 |
| College of Liberal Arts ....... | 1,140 | 16 | 33 | 41 | 10 |
| Private liberal arts colleges ..... | 875 | 20 | 43 | 33 | 4 |
| Catholic women's colleges ....... | 492 | 18 | 36 | 39 | 7 |
| State colleges ................. | 1,133 | 15 | 34 | 41 | 10 |
| Junior colleges ................. | 462 | 23 | 35 | 34 | 8 |

10–15 percent of the boys expected to receive no help from their families as compared with 4–10 percent of the girls.

It should be emphasized that although students responded similarly in each of the different types of colleges, the cost of attending each of the different types of colleges varies widely. At the junior colleges where most of the students would be living at home and commuting, tuition is only $200 per year and other costs are nominal. At the private liberal arts colleges, on the other hand, most of the students would be living on the campus, and their total expenses would be $2,000 to $3,000 per year. With this very wide range in total college costs, the fact that the extent of family help at each of the different types of colleges was similar was an unexpected finding. The proportion of boys, for example, checking the phrase "Pay some of my expenses" ranges only from 45 percent of the boys in the junior colleges to 50 percent of those in the private liberal arts colleges. The proportion of college costs the student expects to be met by his family remained constant even though the actual costs vary greatly. These data were, of course, gathered while the students were in their senior year of high school and before they were actually faced with any of the costs of attending college, so the students' expectations may not have been realistic.

## Books in the Home

College students come from all types of cultural backgrounds. One of the questionnaire items related to cultural background asked the students to indicate the number of books their families had in their homes. The students checked various categories ranging from fewer than 10 books at home to more than 100 books. A surprisingly high proportion of college freshmen checked the two smallest categories — 0–9 and 10–24 books in the home. Approximately 2 percent of the freshmen indicated they came from homes where there were fewer than 10 books. For each of the types of liberal arts colleges and in the university's Institute of Technology, the percentages of students reporting fewer than 25 books in their homes ranged from 5 percent to 9 percent. For men in the university's College of Agriculture and for students of both sexes in the junior colleges and state colleges, 15–18 percent reported fewer than 25 books in their homes. Approximately half of the students in the liberal arts colleges in the state reported more than 100 books in their homes as compared with less than 30 percent of the students in the state and junior colleges.

Table 12. Percentage of Freshmen at Different Types of Minnesota
Colleges by Reported Number of Books in Home

| Type of College | No. of Freshmen | 0–9 | 10–24 | 25–49 | 50–99 | 100 or more |
|---|---|---|---|---|---|---|
| | *Men* | | | | | |
| University of Minnesota | | | | | | |
| College of Agriculture ........ | 227 | 2% | 13% | 30% | 26% | 28% |
| Institute of Technology ....... | 606 | 1 | 8 | 22 | 28 | 42 |
| College of Liberal Arts ....... | 1,172 | 1 | 6 | 15 | 28 | 50 |
| Private liberal arts colleges ..... | 830 | 1 | 7 | 15 | 25 | 52 |
| Catholic men's colleges ......... | 647 | 1 | 7 | 19 | 30 | 43 |
| State colleges .................. | 854 | 4 | 13 | 26 | 28 | 28 |
| Junior colleges ................. | 1,461 | 3 | 14 | 28 | 30 | 26 |
| | *Women* | | | | | |
| University of Minnesota | | | | | | |
| College of Agriculture ........ | 152 | 1 | 7 | 22 | 34 | 38 |
| Institute of Technology ....... | 10 | 0 | 0 | 10 | 10 | 80 |
| College of Liberal Arts ....... | 1,214 | 1 | 6 | 18 | 30 | 46 |
| Private liberal arts colleges ..... | 897 | 0 | 5 | 18 | 28 | 48 |
| Catholic women's colleges ....... | 535 | 2 | 7 | 21 | 30 | 40 |
| State colleges .................. | 593 | 3 | 14 | 25 | 31 | 28 |
| Junior colleges ................. | 1,333 | 5 | 13 | 27 | 28 | 27 |

For all of the entering freshmen in the state, 2 percent reported fewer
than 10 books in their homes, 10 percent reported 10–24 books, 22 percent reported 25–49 books, 29 percent reported between 50 and 100
books. *As a group the total population of college freshmen did not come
from particularly "bookish" homes.* These figures are in sharp contrast
to those usually found in the typical Ivy League institution where perhaps 5 percent of the students have fewer than 50 books in their homes
and 20 percent have over 1,000.

## Plans for Graduate or Professional Training

The numbers of students entering graduate and professional training
beyond the typical four years of college have increased rapidly during
the past twenty years. Now over two-thirds of the seniors who obtain
bachelor's degrees from the colleges and universities in this country
plan to undertake some type of graduate or professional training (Davis, 1962). Students in this study were asked, while they were still high
school seniors, if they had any plans for further training after their undergraduate college work. A substantial proportion even at this early
date indicated that they were planning to continue their education beyond the undergraduate degree. The proportions reporting such plans
are shown for each of the types of colleges in Table 13. *The figures in this*

Table 13. Percentage of Freshmen at Different Types of Minnesota Colleges
Planning to Attend Graduate or Professional School

| Type of College | Number Answering Item | Percentage Considering Graduate School |
|---|---|---|
| *Men* | | |
| University of Minnesota | | |
| College of Agriculture ............. | 156 | 24 |
| Institute of Technology ............ | 384 | 40 |
| General College ................... | 290 | 19 |
| College of Liberal Arts ............ | 619 | 37 |
| Private liberal arts colleges .......... | 489 | 47 |
| Catholic men's colleges ............. | 360 | 33 |
| State colleges ...................... | 840 | 19 |
| Junior colleges ..................... | 575 | 25 |
| *Women* | | |
| University of Minnesota | | |
| College of Agriculture ............. | 119 | 14 |
| Institute of Technology ........... | 5 | 40 |
| General College ................... | 143 | 13 |
| College of Liberal Arts ............ | 873 | 20 |
| Private liberal arts colleges .......... | 693 | 22 |
| Catholic women's colleges ............ | 370 | 21 |
| State colleges ...................... | 903 | 13 |
| Junior colleges ..................... | 387 | 11 |

table show large differences in postgraduate plans among students attending the different types of colleges. Students who planned graduate work were proportionally twice as numerous in private liberal arts colleges as in state or junior colleges or in the university's College of Agriculture. Almost half of the boys who entered the private liberal arts colleges had such plans. The proportions of girls with plans for education beyond college were considerably smaller than for the boys. *The proportion of girls planning on graduate work in each of the different types of colleges was approximately one-half that for the boys.* Like the boys, girls in the private liberal arts colleges were considerably more likely to have plans for graduate study than were girls in other types of colleges.

The large numbers of college graduates with plans for further degrees have led to the less-than-serious remark that "if college training is doing nothing else well, it is doing a good job of selling students on the need for additional college training." These results suggest that colleges may be merely maintaining a high interest in graduate training that has already been developed before college entrance.

Approximately one-third of the entering freshmen in this study had plans for graduate or professional training while approximately two-thirds of the graduating seniors in Davis' study had such plans. Since almost half of the entering freshmen students will not graduate from college, it can probably be assumed that students who as entering freshmen had plans for graduate study are more likely to be found among the graduates than among the dropouts. Thus the majority of college seniors with plans for further training may have at least made tentative plans for this training while still in high school — before they had even begun their college careers.

### Plans for Marriage

The students were asked if they had any idea when they planned to get married and those who had such plans were asked when this marriage was likely to occur. The proportions of students checking each of the categories under this item are shown in Table 14. *Few students had any specific marriage plans at this time.* Approximately one-fifth of the boys and one-third of the girls were considering marriage during the next several years. *Although it might be expected that girls who chose to attend a two-year junior college would be more likely to have more immediate plans than those attending a four-year college, the figures do*

Table 14. Percentage of Freshmen at Different Types of Minnesota Colleges Reporting When They Plan to Marry

| Type of College | No. of Freshmen | Next Year | In a Few Years | Can't Say | Not Planning on Marriage |
|---|---|---|---|---|---|
| | | *Men* | | | |
| University of Minnesota | | | | | |
| College of Agriculture .... | 229 | 0% | 21% | 69% | 10% |
| Institute of Technology .. | 613 | 0 | 20 | 69 | 10 |
| General College .......... | 547 | 0 | 19 | 63 | 18 |
| College of Liberal Arts ... | 1,188 | 0 | 20 | 66 | 14 |
| Private liberal arts colleges.. | 826 | 0 | 21 | 68 | 12 |
| Catholic men's colleges ..... | 650 | 0 | 18 | 68 | 14 |
| State colleges .............. | 1,463 | 0 | 23 | 64 | 12 |
| Junior colleges ............. | 857 | 0 | 19 | 65 | 15 |
| | | *Women* | | | |
| University of Minnesota | | | | | |
| College of Agriculture .... | 152 | 2 | 42 | 51 | 5 |
| Institute of Technology .. | 10 | 0 | 20 | 60 | 20 |
| General College .......... | 242 | 0 | 41 | 51 | 8 |
| College of Liberal Arts.... | 1,225 | 1 | 31 | 60 | 8 |
| Private liberal arts colleges .. | 902 | 1 | 32 | 61 | 6 |
| Catholic women's colleges ... | 536 | 0 | 24 | 60 | 15 |
| State colleges .............. | 1,342 | 0 | 29 | 64 | 7 |
| Junior colleges ............. | 592 | 1 | 29 | 57 | 13 |

*not show such differences.* The girls attending the university's two-year General College and those in the university's College of Agriculture (most of whom major in home economics) were somewhat more likely than others to have earlier marriage plans. Several of the Catholic women's colleges had higher proportions of girls who said they were "not planning on marriage," perhaps reflecting the fact that a portion of girls in such colleges plan to become nuns.

## The Relationship of Socioeconomic Factors to Achievement in College

In addition to comparing students who entered different types of colleges on the various socioeconomic variables, it was also possible to study the relationship of each of these variables to academic achievement as measured by college grade-point average in different colleges. In this way it was possible to determine if students from particular types of backgrounds were more likely to meet with greater success in one type of college as compared with another.

The relationship of a number of the socioeconomic variables to achievement in college was examined by computing zero-order correlation coefficients and multiple correlation coefficients for students of each sex. Multiple correlation coefficients were computed for six socioeconomic variables in addition to high school rank and scholastic aptitude test score. In this way the relationship of socioeconomic factors to college achievement could be compared in each type of college both with and without the control of previous achievement as measured by high school rank and ability as measured by the scholastic aptitude test scores.

Zero-order correlations are presented for each of the socioeconomic variables in Table 15. In most cases socioeconomic variables were not significantly related to academic achievement in college. When significant relationships did exist, they were of a very small magnitude ranging from approximately .1 to .2.

Parental educational level was significantly related to achievement in the university's College of Liberal Arts and in the iron range junior colleges. When student ability was controlled, parental education remained significantly related to achievement only in the case of men in the university's College of Liberal Arts, in which case it was the educational level of the mother which was related to academic achievement.

The students' reports of the adequacy of their family income and the

Table 15. Comparison of Correlation Coefficients between Socioeconomic Variables and Student Achievement at Different Types of Minnesota Colleges

| Type of College | No. of Freshmen | Father's Education | Mother's Education | Adequacy of Income | Family Help with College Expenses | Family Feelings about College | Number of Books in Home | Live on Farm |
|---|---|---|---|---|---|---|---|---|
| **Men** | | | | | | | | |
| University of Minnesota | | | | | | | | |
| College of Agriculture ... | 166 | −.10 | −.02 | −.06 | .12 | −.04 | −.09 | .22† |
| Institute of Technology ... | 464 | .01 | .04 | −.05 | −.02 | −.08 | .00 | .04 |
| College of Liberal Arts ... | 836 | .07* | .13† | −.01 | −.04 | −.01 | .06 | .06 |
| Private liberal arts colleges. | 409 | .03 | .04 | −.09 | .08 | .03 | .01 | −.03 |
| Catholic men's colleges ..... | 511 | −.10* | −.08 | −.12† | .09* | .04 | −.01 | .06 |
| State colleges ............. | 1,084 | −.05 | −.01 | −.10† | .13† | .00 | −.04 | .05 |
| Iron range junior colleges ... | 318 | .16† | .17† | −.08 | −.05 | −.06 | .06 | .02 |
| Other junior colleges ....... | 292 | .02 | .08 | .03 | .04 | .04 | −.04 | .09 |
| **Women** | | | | | | | | |
| University of Minnesota | | | | | | | | |
| College of Agriculture ..... | 121 | −.05 | −.01 | .09 | .09 | .14 | .08 | .11 |
| College of Liberal Arts..... | 916 | .04 | .09† | .02 | .00 | .01 | .07* | .06 |
| Private liberal arts colleges.. | 478 | .03 | .03 | −.09* | .20† | .04 | .02 | .05 |
| Catholic women's colleges... | 399 | −.01 | −.02 | −.07 | .20† | .17† | −.06 | .03 |
| State colleges ............. | 1,014 | −.05 | −.01 | −.11† | .18† | .02 | .03 | .14† |
| Iron range junior colleges ... | 212 | .15* | .08 | −.03 | .09 | .06 | .10 | −.10 |
| Other junior colleges ....... | 174 | .03 | .10 | −.04 | −.05 | .01 | .05 | .07 |

* Significant at .05 level.
† Significant at .01 level.

42

extent to which they felt their families would help meet their college expenses were related to academic achievement for students in Catholic colleges and state colleges, and for women in private liberal arts colleges. (On the item dealing with the adequacy of family income, students checked one of six descriptions of family income ranging from "frequently have difficulty making ends meet" to "wealthy.") The negative correlation indicates a slight tendency for students from lower income levels to obtain higher grades in college. The significant correlations found between extent of family financial help and academic achievement in college were positive. This positive relationship indicated that students expecting to receive smaller amounts of financial help from their families tended to achieve slightly better grades in these colleges. Therefore, on both of these items students from lower socioeconomic backgrounds obtained slightly higher grades in certain colleges. The reason for this relationship in the private liberal arts colleges and the Catholic women's colleges perhaps is that girls from less affluent homes would not have been able to attend the more expensive colleges had they not received scholarship aid. These were undoubtedly bright girls with excellent high school records who continued to achieve high grades in college. A fact which supports this hypothesis is that these socioeconomic items no longer contributed to the prediction of college achievement when high school ranks and test scores were included in a regression equation.

The number of books in the home is an example of a type of socioeconomic and cultural factor which has been found to be significantly related to whether or not a student decides to attend college. In this chapter it was shown to be slightly related to the type of college that the student chose to attend, but was found to be completely unrelated to achievement in any of the various types of colleges. The reported family attitude toward college (measured on the questionnaire by five items ranging from "Insists that I go" to "Won't allow me to go") was also found to be unrelated to college achievement in most cases.

Whether or not the student had lived on a farm was found to be related to college achievement in the College of Agriculture at the university. This variable was also related to grades of students in other types of colleges in a rather interesting way. Therefore, one of the later chapters will be devoted to an examination of the academic achievement in college of students from farm backgrounds.

A number of different variables can be combined to predict college

Table 16. Comparison of Multiple Correlation Coefficients between Several Socioeconomic Variables and Student Achievement at Different Types of Minnesota Colleges

| Type of College | No. of Freshmen | Socioeconomic Variables | | High School Rank and MSAT | | High School Rank, MSAT, and Socioeconomic Variables | |
|---|---|---|---|---|---|---|---|
| | | Total Group r | Median r | Total Group r | Median r | Total Group r | Median r |
| *Men* | | | | | | | |
| University of Minnesota | | | | | | | |
| College of Agriculture | 166 | .26 | | .68 | | .69 | |
| Institute of Technology | 464 | .09 | | .58 | | .58 | |
| College of Liberal Arts | 774 | .18 | | .48 | | .50 | |
| Private liberal arts colleges | 409 | .13 | .35 | .60 | .61 | .61 | .67 |
| Catholic men's colleges | 511 | .16 | .27 | .60 | .57 | .61 | .61 |
| State colleges | 1,084 | .15 | .27 | .61 | .60 | .61 | .64 |
| Iron range junior colleges | 318 | .23 | .39 | .69 | .71 | .70 | .78 |
| Other junior colleges | 292 | .17 | .34 | .60 | .64 | .61 | .73 |
| *Women* | | | | | | | |
| University of Minnesota | | | | | | | |
| College of Agriculture | 121 | .26 | | .77 | | .79 | |
| College of Liberal Arts | 806 | .19 | | .56 | | .57 | |
| Private liberal arts colleges | 478 | .22 | .39 | .62 | .60 | .63 | .68 |
| Catholic women's colleges | 399 | .24 | .39 | .68 | .74 | .68 | .78 |
| State colleges | 1,014 | .24 | .34 | .74 | .74 | .74 | .78 |
| Iron range junior colleges | 212 | .22 | .42 | .67 | .76 | .68 | .81 |
| Other junior colleges | 174 | .15 | .39 | .59 | .67 | .60 | .72 |

grades through the computation of multiple correlation coefficients. Multiple correlation coefficients were computed between all six socioeconomic variables discussed above and achievement in college. These coefficients fall in the general range of .1 to .25, indicating that even when taken in combination, these variables account for less than 6 percent of the variability in college achievement. The median multiple correlation coefficients obtained between these six variables and achievement at individual colleges within each type are also shown. In general the coefficients obtained for individual colleges are considerably higher than those obtained for the total group, ranging in the vicinity of .3 to .4.

For purposes of comparison, the multiple correlation coefficients obtained from using high school rank and scholastic aptitude test score are also given in Table 16. For each of the different types of colleges, the magnitude of the multiple correlation coefficients obtained for the six socioeconomic variables in no way compares with the considerably greater magnitude of those obtained from high school achievement and test scores.

Table 16 also shows the multiple correlation coefficients obtained when all these variables — high school rank, scholastic aptitude test, and the six socioeconomic variables — are combined in a multiple regression equation. The coefficients obtained with this equation using eight variables can be compared with those using just the two — high school rank and MSAT — to examine the extent to which socioeconomic variables add to high school rank and test score variables in the prediction of college achievement. *This comparison indicates that for each of the different types of colleges, socioeconomic variables add virtually nothing to the prediction of college achievement that can be obtained from high school ranks and scholastic aptitude test scores alone.* Not only is this true for each type of college but in most cases it is also true for individual colleges.

Chapter 5

# THE ACADEMIC ACHIEVEMENT OF WORKING-CLASS STUDENTS

THE PREVIOUS chapter reported the differences among various types of colleges in the socioeconomic backgrounds of their students and the general relationship of socioeconomic variables to college achievement. In this chapter the academic achievement of students from two specific socioeconomic backgrounds — those from unskilled laborer and from skilled trade families — is examined at different types of institutions.

On most college campuses, students from lower-class backgrounds are in a distinct minority and middle-class values and attitudes prevail. These differences in attitudes and values may affect scholastic achievement, and perhaps differentially at different colleges. College students from lower-class social backgrounds may be more vocationally oriented than other students. If that is so, lower-class students enrolled in a liberal arts college might find course work less congruent with their attitudes than lower-class students at a junior college or engineering college would, with the result that their achievement would be lower. Lack of cultural background might make a difference in achievement of lower-class students on all campuses or only in selective colleges. On the other hand, since fewer lower-class students attend college, the additional motivation required for those who do could result in higher achievement on most campuses.

Therefore, several of the variables included in this study were examined to determine relationships between working-class backgrounds and achievement in college. Students who indicated on the questionnaire that their fathers were unskilled laborers or unskilled factory workers were examined as one group and those who indicated that their fathers were skilled tradesmen as another. Mean grade-point averages, high school ranks, test scores, and personality scores for each of these socioeconomic groups were compared with those for the total entering freshman class at each type of college.

## Students from Unskilled Laborer Backgrounds

*Academic Achievement.* The college achievement of students from families of unskilled laborers and their mean high school rank and mean test scores are compared with those of the total student body in each type of college in Minnesota in Table 17. Students in the university's College of Agriculture were not included in this analysis because there were only a few such students in that college. *The data show no consistent patterns of college achievement across the different types of colleges for students of either sex whose fathers were unskilled laborers.*

Table 17. Comparison of Means and Correlations of Grade-Point Averages, High School Ranks, and Minnesota Scholastic Aptitude Test Scores for Freshmen from Unskilled Laborer (UL) Backgrounds and All Freshmen at Different Types of Minnesota Colleges

| Type of College | No. of Freshmen | Mean GPA | Mean HSR | GPA-HSR Correlations | Mean MSAT | GPA-MSAT Correlations |
|---|---|---|---|---|---|---|
| *Men* | | | | | | |
| University of Minnesota | | | | | | |
| General College | | | | | | |
|   All ............... | 359 | 1.84 | 34.2† | .33 | 25.0* | .19 |
|   UL ............... | 66 | 1.79 | 40.9 | .47 | 23.3 | .35 |
| Institute of Technology | | | | | | |
|   All ............... | 464 | 1.96 | 81.3† | .55 | 46.2† | .39 |
|   UL ............... | 72 | 1.98 | 75.6 | .30 | 42.1 | .34 |
| College of Liberal Arts | | | | | | |
|   All ............... | 879 | 1.93† | 71.6† | .39 | 43.6† | .31 |
|   UL ............... | 185 | 1.78 | 75.5 | .44 | 41.6 | .33 |
| Private liberal arts colleges | | | | | | |
|   All ................. | 409 | 2.18 | 73.4 | .58 | 43.0 | .43 |
|   UL ................. | 59 | 2.07 | 73.9 | .53 | 43.4 | .39 |
| Catholic men's colleges | | | | | | |
|   All ................. | 511 | 2.09 | 67.8† | .58 | 42.1 | .40 |
|   UL ................. | 61 | 2.17 | 74.3 | .55 | 42.6 | .43 |
| State colleges | | | | | | |
|   All ................. | 1,084 | 1.92 | 53.1* | .60 | 31.9 | .43 |
|   UL ................. | 146 | 1.93 | 57.8 | .57 | 32.9 | .38 |
| Iron range junior colleges | | | | | | |
|   All ................. | 318 | 2.01 | 53.6* | .69 | 34.4* | .44 |
|   UL ................. | 131 | 1.90 | 50.1 | .67 | 32.5 | .46 |
| Other junior colleges | | | | | | |
|   All ................. | 292 | 1.91† | 57.0* | .59 | 34.4† | .38 |
|   UL ................. | 77 | 1.73 | 51.3 | .65 | 31.2 | .46 |

* Significant at .05 level.     † Significant at .01 level.

Table 17 — Continued

| Type of College | No. of Freshmen | Mean GPA | Mean HSR | GPA-HSR Correlations | Mean MSAT | GPA-MSAT Correlations |
|---|---|---|---|---|---|---|
| | | *Women* | | | | |
| University of Minnesota | | | | | | |
| General College | | | | | | |
| All | 166 | 1.77 | 36.3 | .39 | 25.5 | .27 |
| UL | 22 | 1.80 | 38.9 | .58 | 24.5 | .38 |
| College of Liberal Arts | | | | | | |
| All | 957 | 2.14 | 79.7 | .36 | 45.4 | .33 |
| UL | 175 | 2.17 | 78.9 | .32 | 44.5 | .44 |
| Private liberal arts colleges | | | | | | |
| All | 478 | 2.38* | 82.5 | .58 | 44.5 | .49 |
| UL | 44 | 2.15 | 83.5 | .55 | 45.8 | .37 |
| Catholic women's colleges | | | | | | |
| All | 399 | 2.61 | 76.8 | .61 | 45.8 | .53 |
| UL | 43 | 2.49 | 75.2 | .61 | 42.7 | .44 |
| State colleges | | | | | | |
| All | 1,014 | 2.26 | 70.1 | .69 | 36.2 | .61 |
| UL | 98 | 2.21 | 69.7 | .67 | 35.7 | .72 |
| Iron range junior colleges | | | | | | |
| All | 212 | 2.48 | 70.5 | .64 | 39.1 | .57 |
| UL | 81 | 2.42 | 69.2 | .63 | 37.0 | .58 |
| Other junior colleges | | | | | | |
| All | 174 | 2.33 | 67.8 | .58 | 36.1 | .41 |
| UL | 26 | 2.36 | 73.2 | .50 | 37.8 | .37 |

* Significant at .05 level.

Girls with this background did not differ from other students in the average grades they received in college except at the private liberal arts colleges. In the liberal arts colleges their grade-point average was slightly lower than that for other girls at these colleges, although their high school ranks and test scores were essentially equal. For some reason this group of girls did not achieve the grades which would have been expected of them from these two predictors of college achievement. In all other types of colleges, girls from unskilled laborer families achieved academic grades in college similar to those of freshman girls from other backgrounds.

A number of differences in the pattern of achievement of boys from the various socioeconomic backgrounds were found among the types of colleges, but there was no completely consistent pattern across different types of colleges. Boys in the university's College of Liberal Arts had significantly higher high school achievement records but significantly lower aptitude scores than boys from other backgrounds. The college grades they received were significantly lower than those of other students. They achieved essentially the grades which would be expected from their aptitude scores, but underachieved in relation to their high school records. In the Institute of Technology, students from laboring backgrounds had both lower high school achievement records and lower test scores than other students. Their college achievement, however, was the same as that of other students so that they overachieved in relation to both predictor variables. In the private liberal arts colleges and in the public junior colleges there were no differences except that in the junior colleges, those from laboring backgrounds were less able students on all three measures. In the Catholic men's colleges and the state colleges boys from such backgrounds again had better high school records and equal test scores compared with other students but received grades in college similar to those of other students.

Although the pattern of achievement varied, in several types of institutions boys from laboring backgrounds tended to achieve grades in college similar to those which would have been predicted from their test scores but lower than those predictable from high school achievements. These results were the reverse of what had been expected. Since these students obviously came from less cultured and probably less verbal backgrounds, it had been expected that they would be handicapped on the verbal aptitude test. Their grades in high school were expected to be a better indicator of their ability to do college work.

One possible explanation might be that low test scores and low college grades are quite unrelated. Low test scores might result from lack of cultural background while low grades in college might reflect differences in attitudes and values. Since male students from lower-class socioeconomic backgrounds are usually vocationally oriented in college, this difference in attitudes and in values might make them less interested in their course work and they might see it as less relevant to their needs than other students. The trouble with this explanation is that those attitudes which affect college achievement should also have affected high school achievement. In any case, in most of the types of four-year colleges, men from unskilled laboring families did not succeed as well in college as would have been predicted from their high school achievement records. In relation to their high school records, they did best in the Institute of Technology and in the junior colleges.

*Personality and Attitudes.* In order to study further this group of students from unskilled laborer backgrounds, the responses these students made to certain of the personality and attitude items were compared with responses of all entering freshmen in the different colleges. Relatively few differences were found.

One of the items asked students whether they would choose (1) a low-paying but secure job, (2) a moderately well-paying, fairly secure job, or (3) a high-paying, high-risk job. In all types of institutions, students from laboring backgrounds were slightly more likely to respond that they would choose the low-paying but secure job more often than the high-paying, high-risk one. Although the differences were small, they were consistent across all types of institutions. Students from laboring backgrounds, then, seem to be slightly more security oriented than other college students.

It was expected that students from laboring backgrounds would report less adequate social adjustment than other college students. Students from laboring backgrounds who attend college would be expected to have values and attitudes quite different from those of their neighbors, many of their friends, and some members of their family. These differences could result in these college-bound students feeling more isolated and less a part of their peer group. The expectation that these students would be more introverted was not confirmed by results of this study. Among the girls from unskilled laborer backgrounds, no differences were found on the social relations scale and among the men, only in the university's College of Liberal Arts did students from this background report poorer social adjustment than other entering freshmen. *College students from lower socioeconomic backgrounds apparently do not feel they have any more problems in the area of social skills and social relationships than do other students.*

It might be expected that since students from unskilled laboring families would have attitudes and values somewhat different from the typical college student, they might be more rebellious and nonconforming than other students. Furthermore, these students from lower-class backgrounds might have to have been more rebellious in the first place to move away from the values of their parents and friends by attending college. On the other hand, since students from these backgrounds are less likely to attend college, only those who adopt the values and attitudes promoted in their school experiences would decide to continue their schooling by going on to college. Students from these backgrounds, then, who are found in colleges might be particularly responsible, conforming individuals.

In general, the results of this study were in line with the latter hypothesis. *In all types of colleges, college men from unskilled laboring backgrounds appeared more responsible and more conforming than other students, in that they obtained lower scores on those personality items from the conformity scale. No differences on these items were found for girls in any of the different types of colleges.*

## Students from Skilled Trades Backgrounds

*Academic Achievement.* In Table 18 the college achievement of students coming from families in which the father was a skilled tradesman is compared with that of the total entering freshman class in the different types of colleges. Only two differences were found. The pattern of

Table 18. Comparison of Means and Correlations of Grade-Point Averages, High School Ranks, and Minnesota Scholastic Aptitude Test Scores for Freshmen from Skilled Trades (ST) Backgrounds with All Freshmen at Different Types of Minnesota Colleges

| Type of College | No. of Freshmen | Mean GPA | Mean HSR | GPA-HSR Correlations | Mean MSAT | GPA-MSAT Correlations |
|---|---|---|---|---|---|---|
| | | *Men* | | | | |
| University of Minnesota | | | | | | |
| General College | | | | | | |
| All ............... | 359 | 1.84 | 34.2 | .33 | 25.0 | .19 |
| ST ............... | 140 | 1.81 | 35.0 | .27 | 24.3 | .18 |
| Institute of Technology | | | | | | |
| All ............... | 464 | 1.96 | 81.3 | .55 | 46.2 | .39 |
| ST ............... | 135 | 1.87 | 80.9 | .55 | 45.4 | .35 |
| College of Liberal Arts | | | | | | |
| All ............... | 879 | 1.93[†] | 71.6 | .39 | 43.6[†] | .31 |
| ST ............... | 182 | 1.80 | 71.2 | .28 | 41.2 | .15 |
| Private liberal arts colleges | | | | | | |
| All ................ | 409 | 2.18[†] | 73.4 | .58 | 43.0 | .43 |
| ST ................ | 93 | 1.95 | 71.9 | .50 | 41.8 | .26 |
| Catholic men's colleges | | | | | | |
| All ................ | 511 | 2.09 | 67.8 | .58 | 42.1 | .40 |
| ST ................ | 106 | 2.03 | 68.9 | .54 | 41.0 | .36 |
| State colleges | | | | | | |
| All ................ | 1,084 | 1.92 | 53.1 | .60 | 31.9 | .43 |
| ST ................ | 258 | 1.86 | 51.4 | .61 | 30.8 | .44 |
| Iron range junior colleges | | | | | | |
| All ................ | 318 | 2.01 | 53.6* | .69 | 34.4 | .44 |
| ST ................ | 122 | 2.07 | 58.2 | .70 | 35.4 | .35 |
| Other junior colleges | | | | | | |
| All ................ | 292 | 1.91 | 57.0 | .59 | 34.4 | .38 |
| ST ................ | 57 | 1.94 | 54.9 | .63 | 34.0 | .44 |

\* Significant at .05 level.          † Significant at .01 level.

Table 18 — Continued

| Type of College | No. of Freshmen | Mean GPA | Mean HSR | GPA-HSR Correlations | Mean MSAT | GPA-MSAT Correlations |
|---|---|---|---|---|---|---|
| | *Women* | | | | | |
| University of Minnesota | | | | | | |
| General College | | | | | | |
| All ................ | 166 | 1.77 | 36.3* | .39 | 25.5 | .27 |
| ST ................ | 48 | 1.83 | 41.8 | .36 | 25.1 | .26 |
| College of Liberal Arts | | | | | | |
| All ................ | 957 | 2.14 | 79.7 | .36 | 45.4 | .33 |
| ST ................ | 227 | 2.09 | 80.2 | .32 | 44.4 | .31 |
| Private liberal arts colleges | | | | | | |
| All .................. | 478 | 2.38 | 82.5 | .58 | 44.5 | .49 |
| ST .................. | 119 | 2.40 | 84.7 | .55 | 47.5 | .48 |
| Catholic women's colleges | | | | | | |
| All .................. | 399 | 2.61 | 76.8 | .61 | 45.8 | .53 |
| ST .................. | 82 | 2.57 | 74.5 | .46 | 45.8 | .53 |
| State colleges | | | | | | |
| All .................. | 1,014 | 2.26 | 70.1 | .69 | 36.2 | .61* |
| ST .................. | 212 | 2.26 | 70.7 | .62 | 37.1 | .44 |
| Iron range junior colleges | | | | | | |
| All .................. | 212 | 2.48 | 70.5 | .64 | 39.1 | .57 |
| ST .................. | 79 | 2.52 | 69.4 | .66 | 38.2 | .59 |
| Other junior colleges | | | | | | |
| All .................. | 174 | 2.33 | 67.8 | .58 | 36.1 | .41 |
| ST .................. | 51 | 2.28 | 69.5 | .62 | 36.2 | .29 |

* Significant at .05 level.

achievement found in the university's College of Liberal Arts for boys from skilled trades backgrounds was similar to that of boys from unskilled laboring backgrounds. In this college these boys had similar high school ranks and achieved lower test scores and significantly lower grades in college than the freshmen as a whole; they underachieved in relation to their high school grades and achieved as would be expected from test scores. The same pattern of achievement was found in the private liberal arts colleges. There were no differences in other colleges or for the women in any of the different types of institutions.

*Except for the differences cited above for men in the liberal arts colleges, the pattern of college achievement was essentially the same for students of skilled trades backgrounds as it was for all students.* High school achievement and test scores predict college grades as efficiently for students from skilled trades backgrounds as for other college students.

*Personality and Attitudes.* Fewer differences between students from families of skilled tradesmen and other students were found in the various personality and attitudinal items than was the case for students from unskilled laboring backgrounds when compared with other students.

Students from skilled trades backgrounds tended to respond that they would choose low-paying secure jobs rather than high-paying, high-risk jobs more than other students although this difference was not as great as it was for those from unskilled backgrounds. *Apparently students from farms and some lower socioeconomic backgrounds tend to be more security oriented and less likely to take risks than are students from more affluent socioeconomic backgrounds.*

Students from skilled trades backgrounds responded to the various social relations items in a way that indicated their social skills and interpersonal relationships were as adequate as those of the rest of the freshmen at each of the different types of colleges.

Men from skilled trades backgrounds obtained significantly lower scores on the items from the conformity scale in several different types of colleges as compared with other students. The types of colleges in which men responded differently included the university's General College, Institute of Technology, and College of Liberal Arts, and the private liberal arts colleges and the junior colleges. By and large the results on this scale were similar to those found for students from unskilled laboring backgrounds. Again, students of lower socioeconomic status who attend college tend to be less individualistic and more responsible than other students. Perhaps if it were not for these characteristics, other influences in their environment would tend to direct them toward noncollegiate post-high-school training, or directly to jobs.

## Summary

There was no consistent pattern of differences in the relationship of college achievement to predictor variables for students from lower socioeconomic backgrounds. The relationship of these variables to college achievement among students from skilled trades backgrounds was similar to that of other students. Boys from unskilled laborer backgrounds had slightly lower test scores, slightly higher high school ranks, and obtained slightly lower grades in college than other students. These boys, then, achieved in college a level which would have been expected from their aptitude scores, but underachieved in relation to their high school records.

Students from lower socioeconomic backgrounds indicated they would be more likely to take a low-paying but secure job and less likely to take a high-paying, high-risk job than other students. They responded to social relations scale items similarly to other students, while on conformity scale items they reported more responsibility and less individualistic behavior compared with other entering freshmen.

## Chapter 6

# FARM STUDENTS IN COLLEGE

ON THE high school questionnaire the students checked whether or not they lived on a farm and all those who said they did were included as farm students. The category was not broken down further, which meant that students from a giant wheat farm in southern Minnesota, a poor unprofitable tenant farm in northern Minnesota, and a suburban farm owned by a professional father employed in the city were all included in the farm group. For these students answers to a number of questions were sought: What is the achievement level of these students in college? How well do scholastic aptitude tests predict achievement for these students? Is the pattern of achievement among farm students different from that of students from other backgrounds? Are they likely to be more successful in particular types of colleges? Clearer results might have been obtained if it had been possible to discriminate among various types of farm backgrounds.

In Table 19 the farm and nonfarm college freshmen are compared according to high school ranks, scholastic aptitude test scores, and college grades. As a group college freshmen who came from farm backgrounds had significantly higher high school ranks than did those from other backgrounds. On the other hand, they obtained significantly lower scholastic aptitude test scores. *On the average, farm students achieved significantly higher college grades than did nonfarm students, thereby living up to their higher high school achievement records. In relation to their aptitude test scores, farm students "overachieved" in college.*

High school achievement, scholastic aptitude test scores, and college grade-point averages are shown for the farm and nonfarm students in each of the different types of colleges in Table 20. Farm students made up only a small minority (less than 10 percent) of the students in the junior colleges located in the cities on Minnesota's iron range, and the numbers of farm girls in these colleges were too few to include in this

Table 19. Comparison of Means of High School Ranks, Minnesota Scholastic Aptitude Test Scores, and Grade-Point Averages for Farm and Nonfarm College Freshmen

| Student Group | No. of Freshmen | Mean GPA | Mean HSR | Mean MSAT |
|---|---|---|---|---|
| | | *Men* | | |
| Farm ............... | 783 | 2.05 | 66.66 | 36.71 |
| Nonfarm ........... | 3,677 | 1.95* | 61.38* | 38.06* |
| All ................. | 4,460 | 1.97 | 62.31 | 37.82 |
| | | *Women* | | |
| Farm ............... | 665 | 2.32 | 78.29 | 39.36 |
| Nonfarm ........... | 2,829 | 2.16* | 75.57* | 40.97* |
| All ................. | 3,494 | 2.19 | 73.66 | 40.66 |
| | | *Men and Women* | | |
| Farm ............... | 1,448 | 2.15 | 72.00 | 37.93 |
| Nonfarm ........... | 6,506 | 2.01* | 66.24* | 39.31* |
| All ................. | 7,954 | 2.03 | 67.29 | 39.06 |

* Difference between farm and nonfarm means significant beyond .05 level.

analysis. In the other junior colleges of the state, the proportion of farm students ranged from 20 to 50 percent.

In all the types of colleges, farm students had average high school achievement records higher than nonfarm students, but equal or lower scholastic aptitude test scores. In all colleges, however, they achieved higher college grades than nonfarm students. Many of the differences were not statistically significant; however, the trend was in that direction in all types of colleges.

At the University of Minnesota the farm men in the College of Agriculture on the average achieved considerably higher grades than other men, while the difference in the College of Liberal Arts was small. As was shown in a previous chapter, only 5 percent of the students in the university's College of Liberal Arts came from farms, while the percentages were much larger in other colleges. The few farm men who did attend this college had records of high school achievement which were superior as a group to other students in that college. The scores they obtained on the scholastic aptitude tests were also higher; however, the grades they received for their freshman year averaged only slightly higher than those achieved by other students. They were not nearly as high as would have been expected from their high school achievement. In relation to their high school records, then, men from farm backgrounds attending the university "overachieved" in the College of Agriculture, achieved as would be expected in the Institute of Technology, and "underachieved" in the College of Liberal Arts.

Table 20. Comparison of Means of High School Percentile Ranks, Minnesota Scholastic Aptitude Test Scores, and Grade-Point Averages for Farm and Nonfarm Freshmen at Different Types of Minnesota Colleges

| Type of College | No. of Freshmen | | GPA | | HSR | | MSAT | |
|---|---|---|---|---|---|---|---|---|
| | Farm | Nonfarm | Farm | Nonfarm | Farm | Nonfarm | Farm | Nonfarm |
| **Men** | | | | | | | | |
| University of Minnesota | | | | | | | | |
| College of Agriculture | 84 | 82 | 2.11 | 1.75* | 68.2 | 60.1* | 36.7 | 38.5 |
| Institute of Technology | 76 | 388 | 2.03 | 1.95 | 84.2 | 80.7 | 45.7 | 46.3 |
| College of Liberal Arts | 58 | 800 | 2.14 | 1.93 | 81.9 | 70.9 | 46.8 | 43.4 |
| Private liberal arts colleges | 112 | 305 | 2.23 | 2.19 | 74.6 | 73.2 | 40.2 | 44.1* |
| Catholic men's colleges | 60 | 451 | 2.23 | 2.07 | 72.8 | 67.1 | 40.3 | 42.3 |
| State colleges | 271 | 813 | 1.98 | 1.90 | 58.6 | 51.2* | 31.8 | 31.9 |
| Iron range junior colleges | 32 | 286 | 2.05 | 2.01 | 57.3 | 53.2 | 32.6 | 34.6 |
| Other junior colleges | 85 | 207 | 2.00 | 1.87 | 60.1 | 55.7 | 35.2 | 34.0 |
| **Women** | | | | | | | | |
| University of Minnesota | | | | | | | | |
| College of Agriculture | 34 | 87 | 2.36 | 2.19 | 82.4 | 74.9* | 39.6 | 39.3 |
| College of Liberal Arts | 63 | 870 | 2.29 | 2.13 | 89.1 | 79.1* | 48.6 | 45.2* |
| Private liberal arts colleges | 132 | 354 | 2.43 | 2.36 | 84.1 | 82.3 | 42.3 | 45.4* |
| Catholic women's colleges | 60 | 339 | 2.65 | 2.60 | 80.6 | 76.1 | 43.9 | 46.1 |
| State colleges | 316 | 698 | 2.41 | 2.19* | 76.1 | 67.4* | 36.8 | 35.9 |
| Other junior colleges | 54 | 120 | 2.41 | 2.30 | 69.4 | 67.1 | 35.5 | 36.3 |

* Difference between farm and nonfarm means significant beyond .05 level.

These differences suggested that farm and nonfarm students in different types of colleges might differ in the relationship between such variables as high school achievement and scholastic aptitude test scores and college grades. A comparison of correlation coefficients between each of these two variables and college grades showed that in almost all cases they were similar for both the farm freshmen and other students. *Although farm students achieved better grades than would be expected from their scholastic aptitude test scores as compared with nonfarm students, the actual correlation between test scores and college grades was the same for both farm students and the remainder of the entering class at almost all the different types of colleges.* The grade-point average which would be predicted from a particular test score, of course, would be higher than for nonfarm students.

College students from farm backgrounds were expected to have obtained considerably higher achievement records in high school than other groups of students. A smaller proportion of high school graduates from farms attend college than do students from most other backgrounds. The fewer farm students who do go on to college tend to be the more able students (Berdie and Hood, 1965). At the same time it had been expected the high school percentile rank would not be as accurate a predictor of college grades for farm students as for other freshmen. Since farm students generally come from smaller schools where rank in class may be a less reliable measure of achievement than in larger schools, it was felt that scholastic aptitude test scores might prove to be better predictors of college achievement for these students. The results, then, were the reverse of expectations since farm students lived up to their higher high school records by achieving higher grades in college.

Several possible explanations might be advanced for the higher achievement records in both high school and college and the lower scholastic aptitude test scores of college students from farm backgrounds. One explanation might be that since fewer students from farms attend college, the farm student who does attend may be considerably more motivated than his fellow freshmen from the city. This additional motivation could result in a higher record of achievement in both high school and college than that for fellow students from towns and cities.

An explanation of the significantly lower scores of farm students on the Minnesota Scholastic Aptitude Test might lie in the fact that their parents have considerably less formal education than the parents of students from towns and cities, have fewer books and magazines in their homes, and often come from less affluent backgrounds (Berdie and Hood, 1965). Their entire environment may be less verbal; this would be a handicap on a test such as the Minnesota Scholastic Aptitude Test, which is almost completely verbal.

The higher grade-point average achieved by male farm students in the University of Minnesota's College of Agriculture might be explained by the fact that students from the farm have a better background in agricultural subjects and consequently do better in the agricultural courses taken by students in that college. Another explanation for this difference might be merely that students from farm backgrounds tend to take different curricula in the College of Agriculture than students from nonfarm backgrounds. Students from urban areas in the College of Agriculture usually select programs in forestry and seldom take programs like dairy husbandry or horticulture. Differences in levels of competition or in grading practices among different curricula might account for the differences in the grades between the farm and nonfarm students.

Counselors and college admissions officers should expect to find lower verbal aptitude scores among farm students at any level of high school achievement than are found for students from other backgrounds. However, farm students do live up to their high school achievement record in their academic performance in college and do not appear to be handicapped by their lower verbal test scores.

## Chapter 7

# PERSONALITY CHARACTERISTICS OF STUDENTS IN DIFFERENT TYPES OF COLLEGES

THIS CHAPTER deals with differences in personality and attitudes of students and the relationship of these characteristics to academic success in the various types of colleges. Some of these personality variables are related to both ability and socioeconomic background; therefore the results reported in previous chapters must be kept in mind.

As was reported in Chapter 2, each of the entering Minnesota freshmen completed twenty-five personality items on the high school questionnaire — thirteen from the social relations scale and twelve from the conformity scale of the Minnesota Counseling Inventory. Significant differences were found between the sexes on both scales. Girls who entered college responded to the statements in a way that indicated they were more sociable than boys, and boys responded in a way indicating they were more often in trouble with their families or with other authority figures than were the girls. Such differences were expected in that they were found not only among college freshmen but also among the total population of high school students (Berdie and Hood, 1965).

Mean scores for freshmen of each sex in each of the types of colleges are shown in Table 21 for the social relations scale and in Table 22 for the conformity scale. Students in each of the types of colleges were compared with the total population of college freshmen by sex. To aid in this comparison, the mean of each college group was compared to the mean of the total group of all Minnesota entering freshmen of each sex by use of z scores (standard deviation units). Positive z scores are indicative of poorer social relations since high scores indicate more social discomfort; negative scores on the social relations scale indicate less discomfort and better social adjustment. High scores or positive z scores on the conformity scale indicate irresponsibility and rebelliousness; negative scores on the conformity scale are indicative of more reliable and responsible

Table 21. Means and Standard Deviations on the Social Relations Scale for Freshmen at Different Types of Minnesota Colleges

| Type of College | No. of Freshmen | Mean | Z Score | Standard Deviation |
|---|---|---|---|---|
| *Men* [a] | | | | |
| University of Minnesota | | | | |
| College of Agriculture ..... | 209 | 4.22* | +.16* | 2.69 |
| General College .......... | 493 | 3.82 | +.02 | 2.64 |
| Institute of Technology .... | 559 | 4.18[†] | +.15[†] | 3.03 |
| College of Liberal Arts ..... | 1,072 | 3.35[†] | −.15[†] | 2.90 |
| Private liberal arts colleges ... | 765 | 3.37[†] | −.14[†] | 2.70 |
| Catholic men's colleges ....... | 599 | 3.50* | −.10* | 2.64 |
| State colleges .............. | 1,384 | 3.90 | +.04 | 2.76 |
| Junior colleges ............. | 789 | 4.20[†] | +.15[†] | 2.80 |
| *Women* [b] | | | | |
| University of Minnesota | | | | |
| College of Agriculture ...... | 145 | 3.34 | ... | 2.51 |
| General College .......... | 226 | 3.08 | −.10 | 2.16 |
| College of Liberal Arts ..... | 1,137 | 3.11[†] | −.09[†] | 2.47 |
| Private liberal arts colleges ... | 849 | 3.24 | −.04 | 2.58 |
| Catholic women's colleges .... | 502 | 3.31 | −.02 | 2.51 |
| State colleges .............. | 1,235 | 3.49* | +.06* | 2.51 |
| Junior colleges .............. | 509 | 3.73[†] | +.15[†] | 2.54 |

[a] For all Minnesota male freshmen: N = 6,348; Mean = 3.769; SD = 2.826.

[b] For all Minnesota female freshmen: N = 5,005; Mean = 3.347; SD = 2.530.

*Difference from statewide college freshmen mean of sex significant at .05 level.

[†] Difference from statewide college freshmen mean of sex significant at .01 level.

students. The means and standard deviations of all male and female college freshmen were determined. Then the mean of each college group was plotted on this distribution and the z scores showing the distance above or below the total mean determined. For example, the Minnesota students entering Catholic men's colleges with a z score of −.10 obtained a mean score on the social relations scale which fell one-tenth of a standard deviation below the mean for the statewide population of college men.

## Social Relations

Men in the university's College of Agriculture reported significantly poorer social relations than students in most other colleges. Since students from farm backgrounds have been shown to be less socially skilled than students from towns and cities (Berdie and Hood, 1964) and since approximately half of the men in the College of Agriculture were from farms, it is not surprising that they reported more social discomfort than other students. Girls in the College of Agriculture did not differ

Table 22. Means and Standard Deviations on the Conformity Scale for Freshmen at Different Types of Minnesota Colleges

| Type of College | No. of Freshmen | Mean | Z Score | Standard Deviation |
|---|---|---|---|---|
| *Men* [a] | | | | |
| University of Minnesota | | | | |
| College of Agriculture ..... | 215 | 1.94* | −.17* | 1.54 |
| General College ............ | 485 | 2.57[†] | +.21[†] | 1.78 |
| Institute of Technology .... | 555 | 1.91[†] | −.19[†] | 1.44 |
| College of Liberal Arts ..... | 1,064 | 2.06[†] | −.09[†] | 1.60 |
| Private liberal arts colleges .... | 763 | 1.95[†] | −.17[†] | 1.50 |
| Catholic men's colleges ....... | 594 | 2.24 | +.02 | 1.66 |
| State colleges ................ | 1,372 | 2.44[†] | +.11[†] | 1.68 |
| Junior colleges .............. | 793 | 2.38[†] | +.10[†] | 1.66 |
| *Women* [b] | | | | |
| University of Minnesota | | | | |
| College of Agriculture ...... | 142 | 1.70 | −.06 | 1.27 |
| General College ........... | 224 | 2.33[†] | +.39[†] | 1.70 |
| College of Liberal Arts ..... | 1,132 | 1.66[†] | −.09[†] | 1.36 |
| Private liberal arts colleges.... | 859 | 1.57[†] | −.15[†] | 1.35 |
| Catholic women's colleges .... | 494 | 1.62* | −.12* | 1.36 |
| State colleges .............. | 1,251 | 1.88[†] | +.07[†] | 1.38 |
| Junior colleges .............. | 514 | 1.96[†] | +.13[†] | 1.44 |

[a] For all Minnesota male freshmen: N = 6,323; Mean = 2.218; SD = 1.641.
[b] For all Minnesota female freshmen: N = 5,018; Mean = 1.784; SD = 1.390.
* Difference from statewide college freshmen mean of sex significant at .05 level.
[†] Difference from statewide college freshmen mean of sex significant at .01 level.

from the average female college student on this scale, which perhaps reflects the fact that the girls in the College of Agriculture come from a wide range of backgrounds.

As was mentioned above, on almost all campuses girls report somewhat better social adjustment than boys. These data show that the difference in social skills between the sexes is particularly large in the College of Agriculture. Similar results would probably be found on many of the campuses of the land-grant colleges where most boys major in engineering or agriculture and most girls in education or home economics. On such campuses the typical girl is probably a great deal more socially skilled than is the typical boy.

Engineering students have the reputation of being much less socially adept and less interested in people than liberal arts students. When the mean scores on the social relations items are compared for the Institute of Technology male students and College of Liberal Arts male students some basis for this impression is found. The mean score for engineering students on this scale is significantly above that for CLA students.

The University of Minnesota is a large metropolitan university with over 30,000 students. It was expected that the more shy, less socially adept students would be more likely to choose smaller liberal arts colleges and, therefore, the average student in the university's College of Liberal Arts would report better social adjustment than the average student in the smaller colleges. Since the Catholic colleges are also smaller than the university and several of them have a fairly cloistered atmosphere, it was expected that large numbers of introverted, less socially skilled students would be found in these colleges.

The data in Table 21 show that these expectations were all wrong. *Men in the smaller liberal arts colleges obtained scores on social adjustment items similar to the university's liberal arts men.* Although the men in the Catholic colleges received slightly higher scores on the social discomfort items than other liberal arts men, the differences were small and not statistically significant. *Girls attending the smaller private liberal arts colleges and the Catholic women's colleges had mean scores on the social adjustment items only slightly higher than girls attending the university's College of Liberal Arts.* Again these differences were small and not statistically significant and could easily be explained by the fact that the university attracts a higher proportion of metropolitan girls who tend to report slightly better social adjustment than students from smaller towns and cities. Even the very small differences in means, therefore, may reflect a difference in residence area rather than social adjustment as a factor in selection of a college. *Smaller colleges do not attract shier, more introverted students than do other colleges.*

Both men and women who attended the state and junior colleges reported more social discomfort than those attending the private liberal arts colleges in the state. Students attending the former colleges tend to have less ability and to come from lower socioeconomic backgrounds than students attending four-year liberal arts colleges and these differences may in part account for their significantly poorer social adjustment.

## Conformity

It was expected that students at the university would score highest on the conformity scale, since the university has an urban environment with a very heterogeneous student population. There is less need to conform, fewer rules and regulations, and less control of student life. Students going to private liberal arts colleges were expected to be somewhat more conforming. Those attending the Catholic colleges were expected to be the most conforming of all, since at the Catholic institutions there is more control and more discipline. Again almost all the expectations failed to be supported by the results.

*The most responsible and least rebellious men were found in the university's Institute of Technology and College of Agriculture, as well as in the private liberal arts colleges.* Men in the university's College of Liberal Arts were only slightly less conforming than these other male groups. Mean scores obtained by girls in the university's College of Agriculture, the College of Liberal Arts, and the private liberal arts colleges were also similar. Both men and women in the university's General College obtained scores on this scale significantly higher than students in any of the other colleges at the university, or for that matter, in any of the other types of college in the state. As was mentioned in a previous chapter, the university's General College is a junior college for students who are less able or who have poor high school records and cannot enter other colleges at the university. The scores on the conformity scale indicate that these students are significantly more rebellious and less responsible than the average student in the other colleges. This rebelliousness and lack of responsibility undoubtedly played an important role in the poorer high school records which made these students ineligible to enter other types of colleges.

On the conformity scale students from the university's College of Liberal Arts and students in the private liberal arts colleges obtained similar scores. *The expectation that the university students would be more rebellious and less conforming than students in smaller church-related colleges was not confirmed.*

*Scores of men attending Catholic colleges differed from scores of other liberal arts college men, but the difference was opposite to that which had been predicted. Students entering the Catholic men's colleges appeared more rebellious and less responsible.* It is not clear why these more rebellious Catholic men chose to attend colleges with more discipline and more control. (These responses were obtained in high school, nine months before entering college.) One explanation advanced was that a high proportion of men going to Catholic colleges attended parochial high schools and there had been something about the atmosphere of these schools which resulted in students obtaining higher scores on this scale. But when scores in such parochial schools were compared with scores in public high schools, no differences were found. In both types of high schools Catholic students choosing Catholic men's colleges were more rebellious than those choosing public institutions. Therefore, a more plausible explanation may be that because of the attitudes and previous behavior of these students, they were encouraged to attend smaller colleges with more discipline and control in the hope that their behavior might be modified by this discipline. Differences were not found among girls in Catholic women's colleges; their mean score on this scale was similar to that of girls in other four-year liberal arts colleges.

Students of both sexes attending state colleges and junior colleges obtained significantly higher scores on the conformity scale than students in the four-year liberal arts colleges, a result which may be related to the fact that state- and junior-college students tend to be less able and to come from slightly lower socioeconomic backgrounds. *It was suggested that students attending junior colleges might be more rebellious than students in other colleges since most students in junior colleges are living at home and it was felt that students who were rebelling against their parents might tend to leave home to attend college. The results indicate that this was not the case.*

## Risk Taking

One personality item on the questionnaire which showed significant differences among students in different types of colleges was that dealing with risk-taking behavior. This item read as follows:

If you had your choice, which type of job would you pick? (Check one)

(1) A job which pays quite a low income but which you are sure of keeping.

(2) A job which pays a good income but which you have a 50–50 chance of losing.

(3) A job which pays an extremely good income if you make the grade but in which you lose almost everything if you don't make it.

The percentages of students in the different types of colleges checking each of these responses are shown in Table 23. Students attending the university's Institute of Technology and College of Liberal Arts were the least likely to pick the response indicating preference for security. Those in the College of Liberal Arts were the most likely to choose the response involving the highest risk. Students in the College of Agriculture were more likely than either of the other two university groups to choose security. The larger number of farm boys in the College of Agriculture may account for this difference since among all the

Table 23. Percentage [a] of Freshmen at Different Types of Minnesota Colleges
Indicating Degree of Security They Would Seek in a Job

| Type of College | Low Income, Low Risk | Good Income, 50–50 Risk | High Income, High Risk | Significance |
|---|---|---|---|---|
| *Men* | | | | |
| University of Minnesota | | | | |
| College of Agriculture ..... | 18% | 49% | 31% | † |
| General College ............ | 18 | 41 | 40 | † |
| Institute of Technology .... | 9 | 46 | 44 | † |
| College of Liberal Arts ..... | 9 | 41 | 48 | † |
| Private liberal arts colleges ... | 13 | 43 | 44 | † |
| Catholic men's colleges ....... | 12 | 39 | 48 | † |
| State colleges ................ | 17 | 46 | 36 | † |
| Junior colleges .............. | 23 | 43 | 33 | † |
| *Women* | | | | |
| University of Minnesota | | | | |
| College of Agriculture ...... | 27 | 49 | 24 | |
| General College ............ | 32 | 52 | 15 | † |
| College of Liberal Arts ..... | 19 | 51 | 28 | † |
| Private liberal arts colleges ... | 22 | 53 | 22 | |
| Catholic women's colleges .... | 26 | 47 | 24 | |
| State colleges .............. | 31 | 43 | 20 | † |
| Junior colleges .............. | 35 | 44 | 20 | † |

[a] For each group percentages do not total 100 percent since a small percentage students did not respond to the item.

† Difference from statewide college freshmen mean of sex significant at .01 level.

high school seniors in the state, farm students were more likely tha others to choose security.

Students attending other liberal arts colleges in the state were mo likely to choose security than were students attending the university College of Liberal Arts. Men attending state and junior colleges we more likely to prefer a low-income, more secure job than other colle men except those in the College of Agriculture. Similar differences we found among the girls; however, most of the differences were of a small magnitude. *Willingness to take risks appeared to be related to the ty of college the student chose to attend. Students of both sexes who a tended the large heterogeneous state university appeared to be mo willing to take risks.* Girls in all colleges were more conservative tha boys. However, in all colleges, the overwhelming majority of studen picked the two alternatives involving the more risk. The college fres men in this study could not be considered to be a security-ridden grou

## Relationship of Personality to Achievement

The relationships between scores on each of the two personality scal and freshman grades in college were studied for each of the differe types of institutions, and the results are shown in Table 24. *Scores on the social relations scale were found to be related to academic achievement in only a few of the colleges.* For men, this variable was most strongly related to achievement in the university's Institute of Technology and College of Agriculture. These are the two colleges in which men showed more social discomfort than men in the various types of liberal arts colleges. These results indicate that in these two colleges with less outgoing freshmen the more introverted students tended to get slightly better grades. Small relationships were found on this scale for girls in two of the types of liberal arts colleges.

*Scores on the conformity scale were significantly related to academic achievement for students of both sexes in most of the types of colleges.* The relationship is a negative one since high scores indicate more rebellious, less conforming students. The relationship between scores on this scale and achievement was particularly high for students of both sexes in several of the junior and state colleges and among women in

Table 24. Comparison of Correlation Coefficients between Personality Variables and Student Achievement [a] at Different Types of Minnesota Colleges

| Type of College | No. of Freshmen | Social Relations Scale | Conformity Scale | HSR and MSAT | HSR, MSAT, SR and C Scales |
|---|---|---|---|---|---|
| | | *Men* | | | |
| University of Minnesota | | | | | |
| College of Agriculture ... | 200 | .23[†] | −.11 | .66 | .68 |
| General College ........ | 451 | .06 | −.19[†] | .39 | .42 |
| Institute of Technology . | 518 | .16[†] | −.09 | .57 | .59 |
| College of Liberal Arts .. | 917 | .05 | .02 | .48 | .56 |
| Private liberal arts colleges. | 466 | .03 | −.20[†] | .61 | .62 |
| Catholic men's colleges ..... | 560 | .02 | −.15[†] | .61 | .61 |
| State colleges ............ | 1,315 | .03 | −.18[†] | .61 | .62 |
| Iron range junior colleges .. | 356 | −.04 | −.21[†] | .67 | .67 |
| Other junior colleges ...... | 355 | .06 | −.18[†] | .58 | .59 |
| | | *Women* | | | |
| University of Minnesota | | | | | |
| College of Agriculture ... | 134 | −.01 | −.30[†] | .75 | .75 |
| General College ........ | 207 | −.01 | −.10 | .45 | .45 |
| College of Liberal Arts .. | 968 | .08[*] | −.08[*] | .56 | .61 |
| Private liberal arts colleges. | 531 | .10[*] | −.10[*] | .63 | .63 |
| Catholic women's colleges .. | 463 | .01 | −.16[†] | .69 | .70 |
| State colleges ............ | 1,182 | .07[*] | −.12[*] | .72 | .72 |
| Iron range junior colleges .. | 252 | .07 | −.01 | .67 | .67 |
| Other junior colleges ...... | 227 | .03 | −.24[†] | .62 | .63 |

[a] Measured by high school rank and scores on Minnesota Scholastic Aptitude Test.

[*] Difference significant at .05 level.

[†] Difference significant at .01 level.

the College of Agriculture. Since significant relationships were found between scores on these scales and academic achievement, the extent to which these variables would add to the prediction of grades based on test scores and high school ranks alone was examined. Results of this comparison are also shown in Table 24. Multiple correlations obtained through the use of high school ranks and test scores alone are compared with those in which scores on these two scales have been included in the regression equation with high school rank and MSAT. The results are strikingly clear. *Although some personality variables are related to academic achievement, they add little to the prediction of freshman grades through the use of high school achievement records and test scores alone.*

## Chapter 8

# THE ACADEMIC ACHIEVEMENT OF REBELS IN DIFFERENT TYPES OF COLLEGES

STUDENTS WITH high scores on the conformity scale of the Minnesota Counseling Inventory tend to be irresponsible, rebellious, and self-centered. In the previous chapter, a moderate relationship was reported between scores on the twelve items from the conformity scale and academic achievement in college. In view of this relationship, it was decided to take a group of students with particularly high scores on these items and examine their achievement in college.

Boys with a score of four or greater and girls with a score of three or greater on the scale were compared with the total freshman class entering each of the different types of colleges. These students responded to the items in a way that indicated they were more impulsive or rebellious than 75 percent of the statewide college group. They could by no means be considered an extreme rebellious or "beatnik" group, but generally were only slightly more impulsive or individualistic than the average college student.

The sample of rebellious students is compared with the total statewide population of entering freshmen in Table 25. *These rebellious students obtained the same mean scores on the Minnesota Scholastic Aptitude Test as did other students. Their high school records, however, were considerably lower than those of other students.* The differences in both high school and college grades were considerably greater for the rebel men than for the rebel women, the women typically reported somewhat less rebellious and more responsible behavior than the men in these samples. It may be that rebellious men behave in a way that is considerably more detrimental to academic grades than do rebellious women.

When the grade-point averages of the rebel students were examined in the different types of institutions, the pattern remained the same throughout (see Table 26). As compared with other freshmen in each

Table 25. Comparison of Rebellious Freshmen with All Minnesota Freshmen on
Grade-Point Averages, High School Ranks, and Minnesota Scholastic
Aptitude Test Scores

| Student Group | No. of Freshmen | GPA | HSR | MSAT |
|---|---|---|---|---|
| *Men* | | | | |
| Rebellious ...................... | 1,120 | 1.74 | 55.36 | 37.27 |
| All .......................... | 4,460 | 1.97 | 62.31 | 37.82 |
| Difference .................... | | −.23[†] | −6.95[†] | −.55 |
| *Women* | | | | |
| Rebellious ...................... | 1,228 | 2.14 | 70.01 | 40.29 |
| All .......................... | 3,494 | 2.19 | 73.66 | 40.66 |
| Difference .................... | | −.05[†] | −3.65[†] | −.37 |

[†] Difference significant at .01 level.

type of college, rebel students had equal ability but lower high school ranks and lower grade-point averages. When the patterns of rebel students in the different types of institutions were compared, the rebel men in the university's Institute of Technology and College of Liberal Arts came closer to achieving grades which could be expected from their ability level than did those in other types of colleges. For the girls, differences in patterns of achievement among types of colleges were less clear.

The socioeconomic backgrounds of the samples of rebel students were compared with those of other freshmen. In the four-year colleges at the university and in the other four-year private colleges, rebellious students of both sexes tended to come from more affluent homes. These differences were not found in the state and junior colleges.

The explanation of why rebellious students come from more affluent homes may be a simple one. Rebellious students from all backgrounds are probably less likely to attend college than are more responsible students. If they come from affluent backgrounds they will be likely to end up in college in spite of this personality characteristic, while if they come from lower socioeconomic backgrounds they will not and may have dropped out before finishing high school.

Rebellious girls tended to come from families where the father had more formal education while rebellious boys tended to come from families where the mother had more education. These differences were not large, and further study is needed to examine possible reasons for this trend.

Rebellious, nonconforming college students had as much tested ability

Table 26. Comparison of Means of Rebellious Freshmen with All Freshmen in Different Types of Minnesota Colleges on Grade-Point Averages, High School Ranks, and Minnesota Scholastic Aptitude Test Scores

| Type of College | No. of Freshmen | | GPA | | HSR | | MSAT | |
|---|---|---|---|---|---|---|---|---|
| | Rebel | All | Rebel | All | Rebel | All | Rebel | All |
| *Men* | | | | | | | | |
| University of Minnesota | | | | | | | | |
| College of Agriculture | 32 | 229 | 1.72 | 1.89 | 60.2 | 63.5 | 34.1 | 36.2 |
| General College | 101 | 359 | 1.62 | 1.84 | 30.6 | 34.2 | 24.9 | 25.0 |
| Institute of Technology | 71 | 464 | 1.88 | 1.96 | 76.3 | 81.3 | 47.5 | 46.2 |
| College of Liberal Arts | 289 | 774 | 1.80 | 1.93 | 66.0 | 72.4 | 44.0 | 43.1 |
| Private liberal arts colleges | 90 | 409 | 1.91 | 2.18 | 69.4 | 73.4 | 42.2 | 43.0 |
| Catholic men's colleges | 99 | 511 | 1.83 | 2.09 | 61.1 | 67.8 | 40.6 | 42.1 |
| State colleges | 291 | 1,084 | 1.64 | 1.92 | 45.6 | 53.1 | 31.8 | 31.9 |
| Junior colleges | 147 | 610 | 1.71 | 1.96 | 47.1 | 35.2 | 33.9 | 34.4 |
| *Women* | | | | | | | | |
| University of Minnesota | | | | | | | | |
| College of Agriculture | 29 | 121 | 1.88 | 2.24 | 66.5 | 77.0 | 37.0 | 39.4 |
| General College | 72 | 166 | 1.67 | 1.77 | 33.9 | 36.3 | 24.7 | 25.5 |
| College of Liberal Arts | 417 | 806 | 2.07 | 2.11 | 77.3 | 79.6 | 45.4 | 43.9 |
| Private liberal arts colleges | 166 | 478 | 2.32 | 2.38 | 81.5 | 82.5 | 45.5 | 44.5 |
| Catholic women's colleges | 96 | 399 | 2.47 | 2.61 | 74.0 | 76.8 | 45.1 | 45.8 |
| State colleges | 325 | 1,014 | 2.12 | 2.26 | 64.9 | 70.1 | 34.6 | 36.2 |
| Junior colleges | 123 | 386 | 2.24 | 2.41 | 62.1 | 69.3 | 36.2 | 37.7 |

as the other students, but both their high school grades and their college grades averaged well below those of other students. The rebellious student attending the university's Institute of Technology or College of Liberal Arts was less likely to carry over his record of underachievement to the college level than the rebellious students attending other types of institutions. Perhaps in a large heterogeneous university professors are more accepting of certain kinds of behavior, or whatever behavior is detrimental to grades is less often practiced or less often identified there. *In any event, rebellious students appeared to achieve more in line with their ability at a large metropolitan university than in other colleges.*

## Chapter 9

# THE ACADEMIC ACHIEVEMENT OF INTROVERTS IN DIFFERENT TYPES OF COLLEGES

THE ACADEMIC achievement of introverted students was studied in a manner similar to that of rebellious students. Students who obtained high scores on the items of the social relations scale of the Minnesota Counseling Inventory were compared with the total group of entering freshmen on several variables. In social relations scores, like those for conformity, large differences separate the sexes; girls report significantly better social skills than boys. The sample of students drawn for this portion of this study therefore included all boys receiving a score of seven or higher on the social relations items and all girls receiving a score of six or higher. These scores yielded a sample of approximately one in five of the entering college freshmen. These students answered the items in a way that indicated they were somewhat more introverted and less socially skilled than the remaining 80 percent of their peers.

The total sample of students with high scores on the social relations items is compared with the total population of entering freshmen in Table 27. In this table it may be seen that the more introverted students of both sexes obtained approximately the same scores on the scholastic aptitude tests as did the total freshman population. Introverted male students obtained approximately the same mean scholastic aptitude test score as did the total group, while introverted women obtained a slightly higher mean test score than did the total group. Introverted students of both sexes achieved significantly higher high school ranks than the total group and also received significantly higher grades in college. *Shy and introverted students at a particular level of ability achieved slightly better grades in both high school and college than did their more sociable classmates.*

Introverted students are compared with the total entering freshman classes in each of the different types of colleges in the state in Table 28.

73

Table 27. Comparison of Introverted Freshmen with All Minnesota Freshmen on
Grade-Point Averages, High School Ranks, and Minnesota Scholastic
Aptitude Test Scores

| Student Group | No. of Freshmen | GPA | HSR | MSAT |
|---|---|---|---|---|
| *Men* | | | | |
| Introverted ...................... | 889 | 2.03 | 64.10 | 38.32 |
| All ........................... | 4,460 | 1.97 | 62.31 | 37.82 |
| Difference ..................... | | +.06[†] | +1.79[†] | +.50 |
| *Women* | | | | |
| Introverted ...................... | 787 | 2.37 | 76.16 | 41.59 |
| All ........................... | 3,494 | 2.19 | 73.66 | 40.66 |
| Difference ..................... | | +.18[†] | +2.50[†] | +.93[*] |

[*] Difference significant at .05 level.
[†] Difference significant at .01 level.

When both ability and college achievement at the different types of institutions were compared, introverted students seemed to do best in the university's Institute of Technology and to achieve no higher than other students in the liberal arts colleges. In the Institute of Technology their test scores were the same as those of other students, their high school achievement records were slightly higher, and their college grades considerably higher than the total group. Chapter 7 reported that boys in the university's Institute of Technology were considerably more shy and less socially skilled than students in most other types of four-year colleges. Apparently, in this college with its less social student body, those who are the most introverted tend to receive the higher grades. In the university's College of Agriculture introverted boys had higher test scores, higher high school ranks, and achieved considerably higher college grades than did other students. No significant differences were found for men in other types of colleges although in most of them there was a tendency for introverted men to have equal test scores but slightly higher high school ranks and college grade-point averages then other students.

Because of these results, a very brief look was taken at the college achievement of a small group of extremely *extroverted* students. The pattern of college achievement (compared with test scores and high school achievement) did not differ from that of other students except for men in the university's College of Agriculture and Institute of Technology. *It was in these two colleges with their less sociable male populations that very extroverted students tended to be underachievers.*

Table 28. Comparison of Introverted Freshmen with All Freshmen in Different Types of Minnesota Colleges on Means of Grade-Point Averages, High School Ranks, and Minnesota Scholastic Aptitude Test Scores

| Type of College | No. of Freshmen | GPA | HSR | MSAT |
|---|---|---|---|---|
| *Men* | | | | |
| University of Minnesota | | | | |
| College of Agriculture | | | | |
| Introverted .............. | 44 | 2.26 | 69.8 | 40.4 |
| All .................... | 229 | 1.89 | 63.5 | 34.1 |
| General College | | | | |
| Introverted .............. | 73 | 1.91 | 36.2 | 24.8 |
| All .................... | 359 | 1.84 | 34.2 | 25.0 |
| Institute of Technology | | | | |
| Introverted .............. | 111 | 2.10 | 83.3 | 45.9 |
| All .................... | 464 | 1.96 | 81.3 | 46.2 |
| College of Liberal Arts | | | | |
| Introverted .............. | 141 | 2.00 | 73.6 | 44.0 |
| All .................... | 774 | 1.93 | 72.4 | 43.1 |
| Private liberal arts colleges | | | | |
| Introverted ............... | 97 | 2.19 | 74.9 | 45.5 |
| All .................... | 409 | 2.18 | 73.4 | 43.0 |
| Catholic men's colleges | | | | |
| Introverted ............... | 76 | 2.09 | 70.4 | 43.2 |
| All .................... | 511 | 2.09 | 67.5 | 42.1 |
| State colleges | | | | |
| Introverted ............... | 182 | 1.95 | 53.7 | 32.5 |
| All .................... | 1,084 | 1.92 | 53.1 | 31.9 |
| Junior colleges | | | | |
| Introverted ............... | 165 | 1.94 | 55.9 | 33.8 |
| All .................... | 610 | 1.96 | 55.2 | 34.4 |
| *Women* | | | | |
| University of Minnesota | | | | |
| College of Agriculture | | | | |
| Introverted .............. | 40 | 2.36 | 79.2 | 40.6 |
| All .................... | 121 | 2.34 | 77.0 | 39.4 |
| General College | | | | |
| Introverted .............. | 24 | 1.81 | 39.2 | 23.5 |
| All .................... | 166 | 1.77 | 36.3 | 25.5 |
| College of Liberal Arts | | | | |
| Introverted .............. | 170 | 2.18 | 80.8 | 45.4 |
| All .................... | 806 | 2.11 | 79.6 | 43.9 |
| Private liberal arts colleges | | | | |
| Introverted ............... | 134 | 2.48 | 88.4 | 49.3 |
| All .................... | 478 | 2.38 | 82.5 | 44.5 |
| Catholic women's colleges | | | | |
| Introverted ............... | 86 | 2.65 | 76.5 | 45.2 |
| All .................... | 399 | 2.61 | 76.8 | 45.8 |
| State colleges | | | | |
| Introverted ............... | 230 | 2.35 | 73.1 | 37.4 |
| All .................... | 1,014 | 2.26 | 70.1 | 36.2 |
| Junior colleges | | | | |
| Introverted ............... | 103 | 2.46 | 66.6 | 36.5 |
| All .................... | 386 | 2.41 | 69.3 | 37.7 |

Among introverted girls, those attending private liberal arts colleges had considerably higher test scores and high school ranks than other freshman women and they also received higher grades in college. Introverted girls attending state colleges achieved significantly higher grades in both high school and college although their test scores were only slightly higher than those of other freshmen. In most of the remaining types of colleges, introverted girls had equal test scores and received equal or slightly higher high school grades than the total group and achieved equal or slightly higher grades in college than the total group.

The introverted group was compared with the entering freshman classes in the different types of colleges on certain socioeconomic factors. The results of these comparisons indicated that introverted freshmen tended to come from homes where the father had less formal education than the fathers of other students. This difference was found for introverted students of both sexes. In general this trend was more pronounced for those students in public colleges than in private colleges. Although they came from families where the father was less well educated, introverted boys reported the adequacy of family income to be equal to that reported by the total group. Furthermore no other such differences were found for any of the other socioeconomic variables. As for the item dealing with risk-taking behavior, introverted students of both sexes indicated they would be more willing to take a secure, low-paying job than other students and less likely to gamble on one which pays better but requires more risk.

Introverted, less socially outgoing students achieved higher grades in both high school and college than would be expected from their scholastic aptitude test scores. Those four-year colleges with the least sociable male populations — the university's Institute of Technology and College of Agriculture — were the two colleges in which introverted students were most likely to overachieve and extroverted students most likely to underachieve in their academic work. Although introversion was slightly related to academic achievement in most colleges, this relationship was not nearly as marked as that reported in the previous chapter for nonconformity.

## Chapter 10

# IMPLICATIONS FOR EDUCATORS

AMERICAN SOCIETY has often been slow to adopt findings which have emerged from psychological research. The establishment of mental health centers, progress in mental hospital treatment, and changes in penal institution practices have not occurred as rapidly as many social scientists would wish. Before such observers become too discouraged, however, they should examine for a moment recent trends in American education. The guidance counselor's principal function is to put into practice psychological findings regarding individual aptitudes and interests, personality and mental hygiene, and vocational development. Thirty years ago, counselors were unheard of in most school systems. Now they constitute an essential part of the staff in almost all high schools, in most colleges, and in many elementary schools. In addition, there are school psychologists, psychometrists, specialists in the treatment of retarded and handicapped children, counseling psychologists, and other specialists who make up an extensive team of applied psychologists from the elementary through the college years. Historians will undoubtedly mark the tremendous growth of the guidance movement that took place during the middle of the twentieth century as one of the most significant events in American education.

One of the many ways in which the University of Minnesota has led in this movement has been in the development of its Statewide Testing Program in which scholastic aptitude test results and other types of information are gathered for each student in the state and made available to both colleges and secondary schools. This study would not have been possible without these data. Similar data are now becoming available to schools and colleges in other regions so that it will soon be possible to conduct many such studies which will yield much valuable information for educators. Some of the implications this study has for educators —

school counselors, college student personnel staff, and other adminis
trators in higher education — are summarized in this chapter.

## Implications for School Counselors

One of the most important tasks of the high school counselor is to
help students formulate plans for their post-high-school education. In
many cases this involves selecting a specific college from among many
of varying types and sizes and making tentative plans for an academic
program at that college. The results of this study again serve to emphasize that colleges differ widely in the ability levels of their student populations and that where a student falls in the range of ability levels at
a college is an important factor in determining what his academic record there will be. This fact is familiar to most school counselors. They
have long made use of whatever data could be gathered about ability
levels in various colleges to guide students in applying to those institutions at which they have a chance of being admitted and where they
have a reasonable chance to succeed if they are admitted.

This study revealed another bit of information which counselors
should take into consideration in helping students choose among various colleges. The distribution of grades earned by students at particular
institutions varies considerably among colleges and universities and differences in these distributions are important in determining whether a
student will meet with academic success or failure.

School counselors help their students make decisions about whether
to go directly to four-year institutions or attend a junior college before
transferring to a four-year institution. Some students plan to attend a
distant small college for a year or two before enrolling at the state university. The information yielded in this study regarding the academic
achievement of students transferring from various types of institutions
to the state university has many implications for this phase of counseling. Students from junior colleges are apparently able to transfer to
certain types of four-year colleges, such as some state colleges and certain private institutions, with little drop in academic grade-point average. On the other hand, students transferring from junior colleges and
certain four-year colleges to the state university often experience a se-
vere drop in grade-point average and for many of these students, the
drop is enough to bring about academic failure. Other studies have
shown that this phenomenon is not confined to Minnesota. Students who
transfer from one college to another need to select their second college

arefully if they have not met with well above average academic suc-
:ess in the first college attended. These findings again emphasize the dif-
'erences in competition students face at various institutions because of
lifferences in ability levels and grading distributions.

Information gathered on the socioeconomic background of college
students indicates that in almost all colleges, a wide range of socioeconomic backgrounds is found among the student body. Counselors
should realize that a student from a lower-class socioeconomic background will find others from similar backgrounds even at expensive col-
eges and, further, that socioeconomic background does not appear to
be related in any important way to academic achievement in any col-
ege.

The counselor should also be careful about his attempts to match col-
eges to the personality characteristics of students. It is very easy for
a counselor to make judgments about different colleges based on single
:ases. He may know a socially extroverted student who attended a col-
ege with a strong fraternity system, got very involved in fraternity activities, and flunked out of the college. The counselor in the future may
attempt to steer extroverted male students toward other campuses. This
study showed that certain aspects of personality were related to achievement in college but, in general, the relationships were similar in all the
different types of institutions. If certain personality characteristics of
a student will either help or hinder his academic achievement, they are
ikely to do so at whatever college he attends.

## Implications for College Student Personnel Workers

The large growth in the numbers of students attending college obviously means that many do not come from particularly intellectual or
cultured homes. This study showed clearly that most students came
from homes with relatively few books and from families where parents
had not attended college. While this was especially true at the publicly
supported institutions, even the more selective and more expensive
private liberal arts colleges attracted many students from homes where
there was undoubtedly little cultural or intellectual stimulation. Living
in an academic community, college faculty members often do not readily
understand the varieties of background from which many of their students are drawn. College student personnel workers should collect this
type of information and report it to other faculty and staff. Conducting
such a program of education about the student body aimed at the entire

college community should be a continuous function of college student personnel administrators.

The fact that students from all types of socioeconomic backgrounds are found at all institutions has other implications for campus student personnel workers. Many of the problems encountered by today's students as well as other aspects of their campus life are not likely to be well understood by many parents. A program conducted by the college designed to inform parents about the goals and objectives of higher education, campus mores, and the problems and pressures experienced by college students — particularly by "normal" or "typical" students — could do much to increase parental understanding and help reduce student-parent conflict. Such a program also could be an important factor in producing a more positive perception of the institution by parents.

There was no evidence in this study that students from lower-class socioeconomic backgrounds experienced any particular difficulty in their academic work on the campus. This does not mean that they do not have special problems. This study did not examine student morale, satisfaction with campus life, or other effects college may have had on such students. There are undoubtedly substantial problems which should not be overlooked by a college staff.

Although there was a great deal of heterogeneity of students at all types of institutions, admissions officers in many private institutions, where tuition charges have been increasing rapidly (in some cases rising from $500 a year to $2,000 a year in less than a decade), must increase their efforts to attract students from lower socioeconomic levels if the institutions are to maintain a diverse student body. Not only will the funds available for financial aid to less affluent students have to be increased, but increased effort on the part of the admissions staff will be needed to seek out students from such backgrounds.

The portion of this study dealing with differing levels of competition and grading distributions also has significance for admissions officers and other student personnel staff. It is believed on most campuses that since a large proportion of the students who meet with academic failure are found in the bottom 15 percent to 20 percent of the entering freshman class, the number meeting with academic failure would be substantially decreased if admissions standards could be raised so that those with the lowest academic standing would no longer be admitted. What is more likely to happen is that the grading distribution in a college will remain the same in spite of changes in admissions policies and the same

umber of students will continue to receive failing grades. It is possible
o change grading practices of a college faculty only with a great deal of
ffort. A few of the more highly selective colleges have been able to make
his shift so that many students receive honors grades and relatively few
xperience academic failure. In most institutions, however, this has not
een the case. In this study a number of institutions were found which
ad raised their admissions standards considerably in their recent his-
ory, but the mean student grade-point average had remained in the
icinity of 2.0 (the minimum required to graduate) on a four-point
cale. When admissions officers are able to raise standards for entrance,
hey must make certain that this fact is well known and fully under-
tood throughout the college. Furthermore, it needs repetition year after
ear since there is turnover among the faculty.

As admissions standards are raised, performance of students who
ransfer to the institution after completing a portion of their college
vork on other campuses is affected. The larger state universities, which
re moving more and more toward becoming junior and senior year
ndergraduate and graduate institutions, may find themselves admit-
ing transfer students who could not meet the standards set for entering
reshmen. Since students coming from different colleges differ widely in
evels of academic achievement even though they have the same grade-
oint averages, universities must establish more flexible requirements
or transfer students — based on the previous institution attended as
vell as the grades received there. Admissions research which has pre-
iously been aimed only at entering freshmen must now be repeated
or the transfer student population.

## Implications for Other Administrators in Higher Education

Mounting pressures for graduate education will place increased de-
ands on universities, particularly public universities. Graduate and
rofessional education is expensive and few private institutions can af-
ord to provide the necessary facilities and staff in many graduate fields.
his demand will have to be met by publicly supported universities and
y public colleges about to become universities. These institutions, now
st beginning to feel some relief from the impact of the bulging under-
raduate enrollments brought about by the post-World War II baby
oom, will now be faced with large increases in graduate school enroll-
ents.

The increase in postgraduate education must also be dealt with by the counselors and staff in the undergraduate colleges. In the past, when a particular department sent only a handful of students on to graduate schools, the faculty members in the department could spend considerable time with individual students, helping them select their institution and generally helping them to cope with the transition from undergraduate to graduate education. Such individual help is less likely to be available today particularly in the larger institutions. Furthermore less information is available to the undergraduate attempting to choose a graduate college than there is for the high school student choosing a college. Undergraduate institutions must provide better counseling for prospective graduate students not only by making staff available for this function, but by undertaking study and research to provide these personnel with adequate information to help them work effectively.

The results of this study showing the large variance in ability level and grading distributions among various undergraduate institutions indicate one of the difficulties encountered in attempting to assess the quality of undergraduate academic work in order to determine which students will be admitted for graduate or professional study. An additional problem is that not only do grading distributions vary widely among campuses, but they vary widely among departments on almost any campus. Certain departments will have courses attracting students of widely varying average levels of ability, but students receive similar distributions of grades in all of them. Furthermore, some departments give large numbers of D's and F's and less than 10 percent A's while other departments on the same campus with students of similar ability will sometimes give over 50 percent of their students A's (often smaller departments or those where there is much individual instruction, such as music).

These problems are intensified by the fact that graduate school admission decisions are made by faculty members within the various departments and not by a full-time admissions officer who might have the opportunity to become knowledgeable about some of these differences. Given the large numbers of graduate students and the complexity of American higher education, certain types of coordination, organization and research relating to postgraduate education are long overdue.

The heterogeneity of students in American higher education poses many problems for educators. In the typical public college, with students having a wide range of ability levels, challenging the able student while still doing an adequate job of educating the less able ones is

•roblem that has been of concern in the past and for which solutions
µust continuously be sought. A number of students from lower socio-
conomic backgrounds for varying reasons never even attempt college;
.igher education cannot continue to overlook this group. As indicated
bove, no relationship was found between socioeconomic background
nd academic success in most colleges.

The heterogeneity of students in American colleges and universities
lso suggests that institutions of higher education in this country should
hemselves remain heterogeneous. All institutions should not aspire to
ecome a Harvard or a Swarthmore. For example, since considerable
µumbers of able students meet with academic failure at certain colleges
nd universities, and since few institutions will accept students who
ave met with academic difficulty at other institutions, there is a defi-
ite need for a number of "second chance" institutions, in view of the in-
reasing necessity of a B.A. degree for young people in this country.
'hese and other types of innovative colleges are needed to provide more
ither than less diversity. The future of American higher education re-
µuires a variety of institutions with a variety of objectives, student pop-
lations, philosophies, and environments.

### REFERENCES

stin, A. W. *Who Goes Where to College?* Chicago: Science Research Associates, 1965.

erdie, R. F. *After High School — What?* Minneapolis: University of Minnesota Press,
1954.

erdie, R. F., and W. L. Layton. *The Minnesota Counseling Inventory.* New York: Psychological Corp., 1953.

erdie, R. F., W. L. Layton, Theda Hagenah, and E. O. Swanson. *Who Goes to College?*
Minnesota Studies in Student Personnel Work, No. 12. Minneapolis: University of
Minnesota Press, 1962.

erdie, R. F., W. L. Layton, E. O. Swanson, Theda Hagenah, and J. C. Merwin. *Counseling and the Use of Tests.* Rev. ed. Minneapolis: University of Minnesota, Student
Counseling Bureau, 1962.

erdie, R. F., and A. B. Hood. "Personal Values and Attitudes as Determinants of Post-
High School Plans," *Personnel and Guidance Journal*, 42: 754–759 (1964).

———. *Decisions for Tomorrow: Plans of High School Graduates for after Graduation.*
Minneapolis: University of Minnesota Press, 1965.

rown, F. G. "Identifying College Dropouts with the MCI," *Personnel and Guidance
Journal*, 39: 280–282 (1960).

ollege Entrance Examination Board. *Manual of Freshman Class Profiles.* Princeton,
N.J., 1964.

arley, J. G. *Promise and Performance: A Study of Ability and Achievement in Higher
Education.* Berkeley: Center for the Study of Higher Education, 1962.

avis, J. A. *Great Aspirations.* Chicago: Aldine Publishing Co., 1964.

•rrest, A. "Counseling Talented Students on College Choice," *Personnel and Guidance
Journal*, 40: 42–47 (1961).

ills, J. R. *Transfer Shock: The Academic Performance of the Junior College Transfer.*

Research Bulletin 64-5, Office of Testing and Guidance, University System of Georgia Atlanta, 1964.

Holland, J. L. "Student Explanations of College Choice and Their Relation to College Popularity, College Productivity, and Sex Differences," *College and University*, 33: 313–320 (1958).

Hood, A. B., and R. F. Berdie. "The Relationship of Ability to College Attendance," *College and University*, 39: 309–318 (1964).

Knoell, Dorothy M., and L. L. Medsker. *From Junior to Senior College: A National Study of the Transfer Student*. Washington, D.C.: American Council on Education, 1965.

Lovejoy, C. E. *Lovejoy's College Guide*. New York: Simon and Schuster, 1965.

Rand, L. P. "Matching of Student and Institutional Characteristics and College Choice Satisfaction." Unpublished Ph.D. thesis, University of Iowa, Iowa City, 1966.

Sanford, N., ed. *The American College*. New York: John Wiley, 1962.

Smith, N. A. "A Comparison of High School Seniors Who Plan to Attend a Junior College with Those Who Plan to Attend a Four-Year College." Unpublished manuscript, Division of Counselor Education, University of Iowa, Iowa City, 1966.

Soldwedel, Bette J. *Preparing for College*. New York: Macmillan, 1966.

Swanson, E. O., J. C. Merwin, and R. F. Berdie. "A Follow-Up in Minnesota Colleges Showing the Relationship of College Grades to High School Rank and Test Scores in the Minnesota College State-Wide Testing Program," *Research Bulletin of the Office of the Dean of Students*, Vol. 5, No. 1 (1963).